Performance Coaching Skills for Social Work

Performance Coaching Skills for Social Work

JANE HOLROYD
RICHARD FIELD

Series Editor: Keith Brown

Los Angeles | London | New Delhi
Singapore | Washington DC

www.learningmatters.co.uk

Los Angeles | London | New Delhi
Singapore | Washington DC

Learning Matters
An imprint of SAGE Publications Ltd
1 Oliver's Yard
55 City Road
London EC1Y 1SP

SAGE Publications Inc.
2455 Teller Road
Thousand Oaks, California 91320

SAGE Publications India Pvt Ltd
B 1/I 1 Mohan Cooperative Industrial Area
Mathura Road
New Delhi 110 044

SAGE Publications Asia-Pacific Pte Ltd
3 Church Street
#10-04 Samsung Hub
Singapore 049483

Library of Congress Control Number: 2011945613

British Library Cataloguing in Publication Data

A catalogue record for this book is available from
the British Library

Editor: Luke Block
Development editor: Lauren Simpson
Production controller: Chris Marke
Project management: Swales & Willis Ltd,
Exeter, Devon
Marketing manager: Tamara Navaratnam
Cover design: Wendy Scott
Typeset by: Swales & Willis Ltd, Exeter, Devon
Printed by: MPG Books Group, Bodmin, Cornwall

ISBN 978 1 44625 673 2
ISBN 978 0 85725 991 2 (pbk)

Contents

V

List of figures

List of tables

List of activities

Foreword

Performance management, whilst key to all organisational productivity, is often poorly executed. Performance coaching combines performance regulation with the unique benefits of coaching to achieve sustainable personal and organisational results. Opportunities to have coaching conversations and coaching as a leadership style are key themes within this text, together with understanding how to combine the best of coaching with improving performance management, which is a crucial agenda for all public services.

This book contains a wealth of knowledge and experience, coupled with a variety of activities, practical examples and tips for success. The skills you are encouraged to develop support and promote a 'learning organisational culture' where staff receive appropriate and timely feedback when it most counts – when issues occur. It discusses how to handle even the most difficult conversations.

It has been expertly produced by Jane Holroyd and Richard Field and offers clear advice and support for how best to improve health and social care delivery via performance coaching. Their many years of experience are clear to see and their expertise in coaching and performance is of real value to the sector. They are qualified coaches and use both their coaching expertise and years of leadership and management experience to provide an invaluable insight into coaching performance.

It is my sincere belief that the text will benefit all who work in this field and, ultimately, their clients.

Keith Brown
Series Editor
Director of Centre for Post Qualifying Social Work, Bournemouth University

About the authors

Jane Holroyd has over 25 years' experience in the development and delivery of services within the NHS and was awarded an MBE for her achievements and services to nursing. She worked for the Leadership Centre where she was responsible for Medical and Nurse Director Leadership programmes and associated links with Europe. She co-authored the strategy document 'Leadership and Management Development for Social Work and Social Care – Creating Leadership Pathways of Progression' and is the author of 'Introduction to Leadership and Management – Improving Personal and Organisational Development'. She is a specialist in developing leadership programmes and organisational development and is a public sector coach.

Richard Field is a qualified executive coach and coach supervisor with over 28 years' experience of public service leadership and management development. Richard started his career as a qualified accountant before joining Anglia Ruskin University where he helped managers develop competence in financial management, planning and creativity. Richard has worked for the Office for Public Management on a number of highly successful programmes including the Future Leadership programme, delivered with Ashridge Business School and commissioned by CLG. Richard, who now works as a freelance development specialist, has an MBA, is licensed to use a range of psychometric instruments and has authored and contributed to a number of leadership development textbooks.

Section 1

Introduction

Welcome to *Performance Coaching Skills for Social Work*, a book primarily for professionals and managers involved in, or responsible for, performance within health and social care settings. The content will also be of potential value to managers operating elsewhere in organisations engaged in public service commissioning or provision.

The current environment calls for the pursuit and maintenance of high levels of sustained performance from individuals, teams, organisations and multi-agency collaborations. High levels of performance require both management and leadership. Management concerns the 'what' of performing – establishing objectives, determining frameworks, processes and systems, monitoring and taking corrective action as necessary. High levels of performance require more than managerial activity, particularly in the service sector where human endeavour and 'how' staff are led is crucial. Coaching, in its various forms, offers a means by which those involved in public service can be supported and challenged to perform.

While this book addresses the management of performance, the primary focus is leadership and the contribution coaching can make to achieving high individual and collective performance.

The content of this book draws on three overlapping domains:

- leadership;
- performance; and
- coaching.

Coaching is seen in many aspects of organisational life, for example, in our spontaneous conversations when a person strives to help another tackle a challenge, discover a way forward or develop a particular skill. It is present as a natural or learned style of leadership and in more formal relationships involving internal or external qualified coaches. In some organisations, coaching is so widespread and embedded that a 'coaching culture' exists.

This book looks at performance through five filters:

- service user;
- self;
- team;
- organisation; and
- community.

The content is intended to be of practical use and includes different ways of looking at performance and coaching, useful processes, techniques and tips. While essentially practical, the content is informed by theory and includes references to other writers in this field.

This book includes material intended to develop a basic understanding of leadership, performance and coaching. In addition, it features:

- activities designed to help you develop skills related to performance coaching and which will cause you to engage with the approach to performance management and coaching within your organisation;
- tips for success, which will help you to get the most out of performance management and coaching in your workplace.

This book will help you to develop competence and confidence in coaching yourself, and others, to achieve and sustain high levels of performance. This will not make you into a coach but it will enable you to have productive coaching conversations and develop a coaching style of leadership.

A coaching conversation is a *focused discussion whereby one individual assists another to achieve their desired outcomes.* Coaching conversations can occur between any two people and are not restricted to situations where a more senior person talks to someone who is more junior. Coaching conversations can occur between peers, can involve a relatively junior person coaching someone who is more senior and can even extend outside of an organisation to include suppliers, clients or other parties.

A coaching style exists *where a leader habitually engages in coaching conversations with those they lead and work.*

This book is informed by the authors' beliefs that:

- achieving and sustaining high performance is the individual and collective responsibility of everyone involved in public service;
- responsibility and capacity for leading performance should be widely held within organisations and the communities they serve;
- high levels of performance require both managerial and leadership competence;
- leaders have a responsibility to make sense of the environment they operate within, to share this with those around them, create a sense of direction and stimulate performance;
- an awareness of self and self-leadership is vital for improving personal and organisational performance;
- the capacity to create resonance in others is vital to leading a high performing service or organisation;
- resonance comes from a capacity to tailor the way we relate to a diverse range of people which, in turn, requires emotional intelligence;
- being able to support and challenge others through coaching conversations is key to high levels of performance;
- coaching others and being open to coaching from those we encounter is a rich source of personal development;
- for coaching conversations and coaching styles of leadership to thrive organisations need a coaching-friendly culture.

Performance coaching through conversation is a relatively new area of leadership, understanding of which is still developing. Reading this text will help shape your thinking, inform your leadership practice and further improve individual and collective performance.

Section 2
Context

This section explores the context within which leaders are required to lead and perform, makes the case for performance leadership and starts to explore the potential contribution coaching can make to achieving and sustaining high performance.

Shifting landscape

The worst recession for decades, rising unemployment and inflation, a new political coalition and significant shifts in public policy after thirteen years of Labour rule create a fascinating context for public service leadership. At a national level, we appear to be witnessing a shift from a top down, centralist approach to public service and performance management towards one that is more locally driven. However, the picture is far from clear and the extent of real shift will take time to emerge.

The coalition has set about reform at a fast pace, sweeping away institutions, publishing bills and taking action that directly or indirectly impacts on performance and performance management. Actions to date include abolishing the Comprehensive Area Assessment process, disbanding the Audit Commission and scrapping a large number of centrally determined targets.

In October 2010, community budgeting pilots were announced with the intention that local councils should find local solutions to local problems by pooling budgets. A number of centrally imposed rules and regulations will be scrapped for these pilot authorities.

The Localism Bill, published in January 2011, introduces new freedoms and flexibilities for local government and new rights and powers, including the community right to challenge local authorities to take on running a service. Also included are plans to make the planning system more democratic and ensure that decisions about housing are taken locally. 'Big society', a significant policy strand of the coalition, is promoted as the means by which local decisions will be made by local people and the state shrunk. Self-help, co-production and volunteering will fill the gap.

In health, there are plans to abolish primary care trusts and make GPs responsible for buying inpatient care from 2013. The Government is introducing the 'right to provide' and public service employers will be expected to accept suitable proposals from front line staff who want to take over and run their services as mutual organisations. These and other changes form the future context within which public services will be expected to perform. The future appears to be one where:

- public services available within localities will increasingly differ to reflect prioritised need and the expressed preferences of the community;
- state-funded provision will be increasingly undertaken by private and third sector organisations;
- provision of services, particularly adult social care, will increasingly be undertaken by family, friends and micro providers;
- interest in comparing outcomes with the initial and ongoing cost of public service provision will grow;
- interest in measuring performance related to commissioning will increase;
- performance measurement will be determined locally rather than imposed centrally;
- performance reward or punishment will be locally determined and administered;
- performance frameworks and processes will be tailored to local contexts.

Performance and the case for performance leadership

Performance is defined in the *Collins Concise Dictionary* as being the 'manner or quality of functioning' or 'the act of performing', which in turn is defined as being to 'carry out an action'.

There are different views as to the purpose of public services and how performance should be measured. Moore (1995: 28), a professor at Harvard University's Kennedy School of Government, considers that the:

> *aim of managerial work in the public sector is to create public value, just as the aim of managerial work in the private sector is to create private value.*

Cole and Parston (2006: 63) are of the view that:

> *public service value is about more than simply attaining outcomes and it is about more than just reducing cost; it is about doing both in a balanced fashion and understanding the strategic trade-offs along the way.*

A characteristic of public service organisations is the number and range of stakeholders involved, each viewing performance in a particular way. Traditionally, these organisations prepare and publish plans that report historic and current performance and set targets for the future. Typically, reported performance focuses on objectives set by the team or organisation which may or may not resonate with services users or the wider community. Where the practice of performance management is effective, individuals can see how their personal performance contributes to organisational targets.

The new emphasis on localities, place-based commissioning and collaborating to meet prioritised community need will impact on how performance is stated and measured in future. This will need to be looked at from the perspectives of service users, communities and organisations.

ACTIVITY **2.1**

Understanding performance in your organisation

Find the most recent plan that relates to your service area and skim read the content. What does this tell you about the following:

- *Key future performance areas?*
- *How current performance compares to what was planned and to that achieved by other similar organisations?*
- *How performance has changed over time?*

To what extent do you think a service user or member of the community will relate to the performance aim and measurement?

The *Manager's Guide to Performance Management* (2006: 8), published by the I&DᵉA (now Local Government Improvement and Development), states that:

> *effective performance management relies on systems and people working together to make sure the right things happen. The hard systems, processes and data are inseparable from the soft aspects such as culture, leadership and learning. One simply does not work without the other.*

Addressing only the so-called 'hard' aspects of performance is a mistake, particularly where the context and challenges faced are novel, complex, contradictory and uncertain. Performance frameworks, systems and managerial competences such as planning, monitoring, controlling and problem solving will not, on their own, guarantee high performance. Performance will have to be led as well as managed; leadership is key to providing the challenge and nurture needed for improvement and sustained high performance.

Situations that are novel and complex often require action that is not knowable in advance. It is unrealistic and unreasonable to expect senior managers to generate every solution to every problem faced by an organisation; it is also disempowering for the staff they lead, cumbersome and short sighted. Throughout organisations, people need to anticipate and respond to the challenges they face; they need competence, confidence and to be motivated to act. This requirement can be demanding for those involved; coaching can be a great support, providing challenge and support in equal measure.

Coaching is a potentially important means of facilitating real performance leadership. It blends opportunities to create an accountability partnership and allows for spotting when there are particular opportunities for growth and development. The result is real time, relevant and applied learning.

Pedler *et al.* (2004: 5) view leadership as three domains, as can be seen in Figure 2.1.

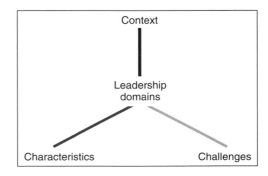

Figure 2.1 Three domains of leadership

Leadership is exercised in a specific and unique local context which is influenced by, and, to an extent, flexes in response to, the wider national environment. As the wider environment and local context shifts, challenges emerge that demand a response. Some of these shifts are predictable and can be met in a timely and thoughtful manner. Consequently, leaders need to be able to make sense of the wider environment, the community and organisational context. Leadership is a performing art where resources are deployed to meet challenges, respond to opportunities and achieve prioritised outcomes.

Characteristics are the leadership qualities and competencies required to respond to challenges within the specific context within which a leader operates. Effective future public service leaders will:

- be aware of the wider environment and organisation, and engage in sense making;
- listen to others, shaping strategy from the bottom, enabling effective and sustained change;
- gather all the information, assess and respond to the risks;
- look to create independence in others;
- create a questioning environment and encourage others to listen;
- promote a coaching culture within their organisation;
- ask effective, and sometimes awkward, questions to help individuals explore situations, challenge thinking and build successful teams, organisations and communities;
- manage conflict and handle difficult conversations.

The three domains model prompts five questions to which organisational leaders should attend.

1. What future wider and local context will we be operating in?
2. What does this context mean for future performance and how will it be measured?
3. How different is this context from the current one?
4. What specific challenges will we face, some of which will be demographic (e.g. ageing population), some wicked (e.g. persistent prolific offenders), others internal (e.g. an organisational weakness)?
5. What characteristics do we need to develop in ourselves and others?

Understanding the context for your performance

Planning documents should be informed by strategic thinking, the outcome of which Mintzberg (1994) considers to be 'an integrated perspective of the enterprise'. Integration involves bringing together insights about many aspects of the service or organisation, including the external environment or context within which the organisation will operate. In order to develop a rich understanding of the external context, it is helpful to undertake an environmental scan.

A number of environmental scanning tools feature in strategic management literature, most featuring a framework that points the user to a number of categories of influence, such as sociological, political, economic, legal and technological (SPELT).

When considering each SPELT category, users should identify influences they think might impact on service users, staff, commissioners, competitors and other stakeholders. As Figure 2.2 indicates, this analysis should be looked at over different time periods such as now, within three years and beyond three years. For each influence, the impact and significance should be described and used to populate an impact matrix, as shown in Figure 2.3.

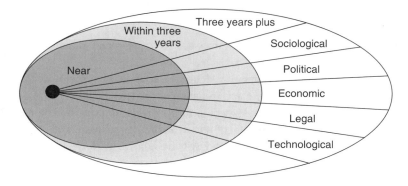

*Figure 2.2
Environmental
scan*

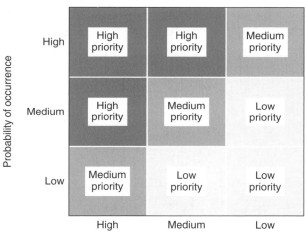

Figure 2.3 Impact matrix

Impact matrices help decision makers identify and focus on influences of particular interest. For each influence, the probability of it happening and an assessment of likely impact should be assigned using high, medium and low scores. Priority rankings can be attached to each cell in the matrix, which helps the user to determine where to focus their attention.

ACTIVITY **2.2**

Undertaking an environmental scan

- *Prepare a SPELT analysis in respect of your service area, focusing on influences that you consider likely to impact on performance.*
- *For each influence, assign a high/medium/low score and create an impact matrix.*

7

Performance, leadership and coaching

The need for commissioners and providers of public services to achieve and sustain high performance is clear.

In future, localities will have a greater involvement in determining which community needs are addressed, and in specifying the commissioning and targeting of services.

All those participating in public service will be expected to pursue community outcomes, demonstrate a commitment to continuous improvement and achieve and maintain high levels of performance. Effective, widely dispersed leadership will be central to high levels of performance. Coaching conversations, coaching leadership styles and formal coaching interventions offer an excellent means of development by challenging and supporting colleagues at all levels to realise their individual and collective potential.

The remainder of this book draws together performance, leadership and coaching in order to help readers develop skills that are fundamental to all forms of coaching.

Section 3

Leadership and performance coaching

The public services, with significant recent changes and grand scale reorganisations, need leaders who see it as their business to take every moment to make a difference. Committed to coaching individuals and actively helping them to achieve, as Kouzes and Posner (2007: 20) state, leadership is about enabling 'others to act'. This type of leadership is not about someone else, a leader by title, who may be charismatic, or an 'informal' leader (someone who chooses to lead and influence); it is not about systems, for we are all individually part of many systems, but about every single one of us. It is about 'self-leadership', a different way of thinking.

Self-leadership

Self-leadership has been defined as 'the process of influencing oneself' to create the direction and motivation needed to perform (Neck and Manz, 2009: 4).

The concept of 'self' is discussed further within the text and is more closely related to the important facet of self-awareness. 'Self' leadership, however, is also linked to the notion of 'dispersed leadership' which focuses on 'self-management' and the positive impact this approach can have upon increasing creativity and productivity (Politis, 2005).

Politis (2005: 186) reports that within self-management there are important additional facets of self-observation, self-reinforcement, self-expectation and rehearsal, which are defined in Table 3.1.

The three factors identified in Table 3.1 were found to have the greatest impact, when tested, upon creativity and productivity, with the first two having the most significance. Interestingly, Hawkins and Smith (2010) in their model of 'transformational coaching' found from experience that practising (the 'action stage') in the coaching session had the greatest impact upon success for the coachee.

Table 3.1 Facets of self-management leadership

Self-observation	Obtaining information and knowledge to monitor own performance.
Self-reinforcement	Recognising and reinforcing own performance.
Self-expectation and rehearsal	Having high expectations and practising a task before performing it.

However, self-leadership is more than the individual equally managing as a form of distributed leadership. It is about changing individual behaviour as a result of changing the way someone thinks (see Holroyd, 2012); implicit in this is the notion of thoughts changing feelings which results in a change in actions and reactions. It is about changing the faulty thinking strategies individuals have grown up with, the script of our so-called 'reality of experiences' which we follow so fervently, even if this creates unproductive states, for example, of anxiety and self-doubt.

It grows from the notion that we take all information from our world through the five senses (visual, auditory, kinaesthetic, gustatory and olfactory) and create a version, or map, of that world in our heads. No two maps of the so-called 'reality' can ever be the same and not just because we all see, hear and feel differently; we also have to distort, delete and generalise information for it to fit.

Our mind and body system is linked. We have a thought and it creates a chemical reaction; we therefore have an associated feeling and our feelings propel us to act and the action has a resultant behaviour. What we are thinking therefore affects the way we feel and behave and is the foundation of habits. Thinking differently can create different actions and different habits.

Self-leadership, therefore, involves, as Neck and Manz (2009) describe, 'leading oneself' using both behavioural and cognitive strategies to positively influence personal effectiveness. Behavioural strategies are those described above of self-observation and would include 'self-goal setting',' self-reward', 'self-punishment' and 'self-cueing'. The cognitive strategies would incorporate examining internal dialogue, beliefs and assumptions.

Importantly, managing your communication would be an integral addition to the above concept of self-leadership. Implicitly, communication, which is made up of the two components of verbal and non-verbal, is the only way we can interact with the world.

This is not about leadership being simply about 'self' but also encompasses how an individual with self-leadership works more effectively within teams, organisations and, fundamentally, within all interactions. Leading projects or work without the reciprocal authority, a more common feature of leaner organisational structures, is a good example of how self-leadership, and the ability to influence others, with intentional communication, can create effective and sustainable partnerships. Managing self is crucial, being resilient an essential leadership ingredient. Remembering that productivity and workplace effectiveness is increased by spending less time, and not more, in the office.

The authentic leader

There is also another important element associated with 'self-leadership' and this is the notion of authenticity and the 'authentic leader'. Kouzes and Posner (2007: 48) would describe becoming authentic as 'finding one's voice', a process of development from knowing 'self'.

Sparrowe (2005), however, would stress that this process is not advanced or independent of exchange but requires continuous interpretation that can only be provided by others. In addition, he suggests that the development of self and knowing self is a constant process with the exposure to different events, people and cultures adding to a refinement.

This sense of continuous learning, and the flexibility to be brave enough to embrace change, ensures that an individual is continuously present in every moment. This creates an unceasing curiosity and the concept of always moving forwards.

In summary, self-awareness, self-regulation and continuous learning are all key to authenticity and credibility as a leader which cannot be developed in isolation and requires interaction with others. Coaching conversations provides an ideal medium.

What about professional leadership?

Within the public services the 'elephant' in the room is often the case for professional leadership versus a generalist model, with the professionals convinced of this being the only leadership approach, and the generalist paradigm not understanding what all the fuss is about. With coaching conversations as a model it accommodates and blends both styles with equal brevity.

Goleman (2000: 1) talks about 'the coaching style' approach as one of six types of leadership. He describes this mode as focused more on 'personal development than on immediate work-related tasks' and also suggests that it 'works well with someone who already knows their weaknesses' and wants to improve.

Arguably, this is only partially true and misses the whole concept and the benefits of tapping into 'self' as the ultimate leadership approach. However, of the six styles (which include 'coercive' and 'authoritarian') coaching clearly has an important place with the other styles described as 'affiliative' (needed when creating a team), 'democratic' (which can result in endless meetings) and 'pacesetting' (which can lead to employees feeling overwhelmed).

One thing Goleman is right about is that a 'leader's singular job is to get results' (Goleman, 2000: 2). However, this is everybody's role and not simply the role of a select few and, furthermore, making it everyone's business is surely far more effective and productive.

Goleman (2000: 4) reminds of the importance of emotional intelligence and, in particular, four 'fundamental capabilities' of self-awareness, self-management, social awareness and social skill. These are expanded on in Table 3.2.

Interestingly, motivation is missing from the list above, which Maher (2001) would add. Many of the above terms are explored and discussed later within the context of the 'coaching process'.

Emotional intelligence is principally focused on the ability to 'self-regulate emotions' in contrast with the above description of 'self-leadership', which focuses on the regulation of cognitive and behavioural processes.

Despite its recognised powerful impact on performance, creating 'real bottom line results' coaching is reported by Goleman (2000: 10) as the least often used leadership style. Even though he advocates using all six styles matched to the situation, the words 'leadership' and 'coercive' do not seem to belong together; or indeed should be in the same sentence.

Coaching as an untapped 'leadership style' works across a whole spectrum of areas from developing oneself, teams and organisations, and stretches far beyond the confines of the organisation into the community, which is effective and appropriate in developing service users to be independent partners. Coaching is not only a 'leadership style' but a conversation and an opportunity.

Table 3.2 Emotional intelligence – a primer

Self-awareness	**Emotional self-awareness**: the ability to read and understand your emotions as well as recognise their impact on work performance, relationships and the like. **Accurate self-assessment**: a realistic evaluation of your strengths and limitations. **Self-confidence**: a strong and positive sense of self-worth.
Self-management	**Self-control**: the ability to keep disruptive emotions and impulses under control. **Trustworthiness**: a consistent display of honesty and integrity. **Conscientiousness**: the ability to manage yourself and your responsibilities. **Adaptability**: skill at adjusting to changing situations and overcoming obstacles. **Achievement orientation**: the drive to meet an internal standard of excellence. **Initiative**: a readiness to seize opportunities.
Social awareness	**Empathy**: skill at sensing other people's emotions, understanding their perspective, and taking an active interest in their concerns. **Organisational awareness**: the ability to read the currents of organisational life, build decisions, networks and navigate politics. **Service orientation**: the ability to recognise and meet customers' needs.
Social skills	**Visionary leadership**: the ability to take charge and inspire with a compelling vision. **Influence**: the ability to wield a range of persuasive tactics. **Developing others**: the propensity to bolster the abilities of others through feedback and guidance. **Communication**: skill at listening and at sending clear, convincing, and well-tuned messages. **Change catalyst**: proficiency in initiating new ideas and leading people in a new direction. **Conflict management**: the ability to de-escalate disagreements and orchestrate resolutions. **Building bonds**: proficiency at cultivating and maintaining a web of relationships. **Teamwork and collaboration**: competence at promoting cooperation and building teams.

Source: Goleman (2000: 4)

Section 4
Introduction to performance

This section defines performance, introduces common terminology, outlines different organisational approaches, explores performance improvement and develops the case for performance leadership.

Performance defined

Collins Concise Dictionary defines performance as the 'manner or quality of functioning' or 'the act of performing'.

According to Martin Cole and Greg Parston (2006: 3) high performing organisations are ones where the quality of functioning is such that high levels of cost effectiveness are combined with high outcome attainment. This is shown in the public service value model developed by Cole and Parston as adapted in Figure 4.1.

The quest for high performance should be ever present. There is no guarantee that once gained high performance will continue. Changes in the environment, increased citizen aspiration and shifts in the relative performance of other organisations necessitate continual performance improvement. High performance as a goal and performance improvement as a process need to be embedded throughout the organisation.

Accounting for public service performance must extend beyond simply reporting money moving in and out of an organisation, activities or indeed outputs. Stakeholders need and want

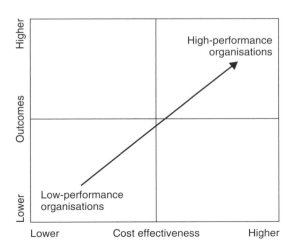

Figure 4.1 Public service value model

to understand the impact of activity and whether this has been achieved in an efficient and economic way, a judgement requiring comparison with previous performance, to targets or with other similar organisations.

Measuring public sector performance is not easy. The lack of a common expression of bottom line performance, the ever present need to control spending and limit taxation and the reality of electoral cycles cause undue focus on short-term performance leaving future generations to bear an unfair cost burden or other long-term poor performance outcomes. The private sector, where profit is a common measure, fares a little better but even here there is a tendency to over-emphasise short-term profit and shareholder return, leading to a failure to consider the wider impact of activity on customers, staff, the organisation, the community and the environment.

ACTIVITY 4.1

Identifying key performance targets

Identify for your part of the organisation the key performance targets.

- *Where are these stated?*
- *How are these monitored?*

Looking at your personal performance objectives, how do these relate to organisational objectives?

The pressure to perform

Recent years have seen many different levers used to stimulate improved performance across the public sector and these fall into seven broad groups, as shown in Figure 4.2.

Market approaches to performance are based on the idea that if private sector organisational forms, relationships and practices are adopted in the public sector then performance will

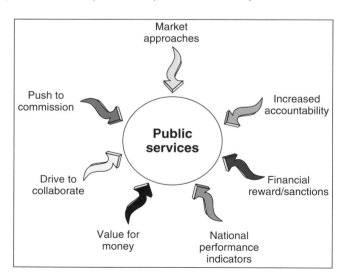

Figure 4.2 Performance levers

be high. The 1980s saw the introduction of direct labour organisations, the establishment of purchaser/provider structures and relationships, widespread creation of business units, business planning and use of service level agreements. More recently, these approaches include market testing, outsourcing, moving services into arms length trading companies and creating social enterprises.

Those advocating *accountability* as a performance lever tend to believe that if local voters, service users and taxpayers are made aware of costs and service quality, and have a means to register their views, this will exert a pressure to perform. The community charge, or poll tax, introduced in 1990 (in England) and measures to increase the quantity and quality of published information via annual reports and tax demand notices, league tables and publicly reported inspections are early examples. Freedom of information legislation and the requirement to publish details of payments over £500 are more recent examples of the accountability lever in use.

Financial reward and sanctions have been used to encourage performance at, or above, specified levels, including grant mechanisms such as capping, unrealistically low inflation settlements, increased/reduced freedom regarding use of resources and decision making, and the setting of efficiency targets.

In recent years, judgements about public service performance have been driven by *national indicator* sets with stakeholders encouraged to compare performance with similar organisations. Centrally determined performance measures and publicly presented league tables pressurise local politicians and managers to improve performance or at least to act in ways that improve reported scores.

Over the last 30 years successive governments have pressed public organisations to pursue *value for money*. The value for money studies, featuring economy, efficiency and effectiveness, introduced in the 1980s were replaced in 1997 by best value studies which in turn were overtaken by the Gershon Efficiency Review in 2004/5. The pursuit of value for money has seen the public sector experiment with a number of initiatives, frameworks or tools such as BS5750/9001, the business excellence model, business process reengineering, service process redesign and, more recently, lean thinking.

While not a new approach, *collaborating* to improve performance between public service organisations has increased since Sir Peter Gershon claimed in 2004/5 that it could lead to potential savings through joint procurement and shared back office services, etc. Total place and, more latterly, community budgeting initiatives have further stimulated collaboration and many organisations are pursuing cost efficiency and/or better outcomes through sharing chief executives and management teams, co-locating services and coordinating approaches to 'wicked issues' such as persistent prolific offending.

Encouragement and, in some instances, a requirement to adopt *commissioning* as an approach to strategic and operational management is a pressure to perform. The requirement to understand the local community and its needs, to prioritise and design responses that are economic and efficient, creates a framework for, and an expectation of, high performance.

At any point in time two or more of these levers are in play, the exact combination shifting with the introduction of new initiatives and the electoral cycle.

Benefits of performance management

Performance management is defined by Michael Armstrong (1994: 23) as a:

> *means of getting better results from the organisation, teams and individuals by under-standing and managing performance within an agreed framework of planned goals, standards and attribute/competence requirements.*

When performance management is done well a number of positive benefits can be expected, including:

- sustainable improvements in performance;
- citizens, service users and commissioners becoming aware of the public value created by activities;
- better decision making;
- the needs of service users being taken into account in service delivery and evaluation;
- staff who are better aligned to strategy and enabled to develop their abilities;
- conversations being prompted about personal aspirations and development;
- increases in motivation and discretionary effort;
- innovation;
- learning which leads to performance improvement.

Basic performance terminology

Performance management involves a number of technical terms, the more common of which are defined below.

Outcome is the term given to the impact an activity is intended to have. Outcomes are achieved through *outputs* in the form of goods and services.

Outputs result from one or more *activities* taking place, each of which consumes *resources* and therefore costs *money*. Three common performance measures are *economy* which, according to the I&D^{e}A, 'means acquiring human and material resources of the appropriate quantity and quality at the lowest cost'; *efficiency*, defined as 'using the minimum inputs for the required quantity and quality of service provided'; and *effectiveness*, defined as 'having the organisation meet citizens' requirements and having a programme or activity achieve established goals or intended aims'. Figure 4.3 shows the relationship between these terms. *Performance measures* and *indicators* describe how well a service or organisation is performing, the difference being that a measure can be directly counted whereas an indicator merely indicates performance. An example for each of these terms is provided as Table 4.1 in respect of a falls-reduction project.

Good performance information

Good performance information has a number of characteristics as identified in *Choosing the Right Fabric – A Framework for Performance Information* published by HM Treasury, the Cabinet Office, the National Audit Office, the Audit Commission and the Office for National Statistics (2001: 11). These FABRIC characteristics are shown in Table 4.2.

When set as targets, performance measures should be SMART – specific, measurable, achieveable, realistic and time bound. Measures should also be relevant to the desired

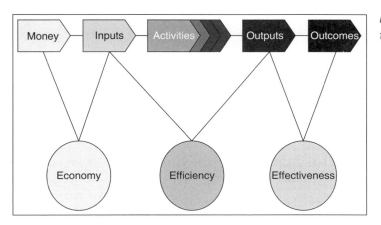

Figure 4.3 Performance terminology

Table 4.1 Terminology – examples

Terminology	Example relating to a falls-reduction project
Outcomes	Including . . . • Reduced falls • Reduction in non-fall-related accidents • Increased service user activity outside the home (going shopping, attending clubs etc.) • Service users feeling more confident
Outputs	• Personal medication reviews • Home safety checks and related minor repairs/adaptions • Exercise sessions
Activities	For safety checks . . . an initial safety visit, a home assessment, ordering and receipt of materials for adaption, adaption visit followed by inspection.
Inputs	Staff and volunteer time, materials for minor adaptions, use of vehicle etc.
Performance measure	• Number of falls • Number of paramedic visits in response to falls • Number of acute hospital fall-related episodes • Number of non fall-related accidents • Client reported activity in the community
Performance indicator	• Client reported confidence score

Table 4.2 FABRIC

Focused on the organisation's aims and objectives.

Appropriate to, and useful for, the stakeholders who are likely to use it.

Balanced, giving a picture of what the organisation is doing, covering all significant areas of work.

Robust in order to withstand organisational changes or individuals leaving.

Integrated into the organisation, being part of the business planning and management processes.

Cost effective, balancing the benefits of the information against the costs.

Source: *Choosing the Right Fabric* (2001)

outcomes, capable of being defined clearly, sensitive in that they reflect changes in performance quickly, allow comparisons and are verifiable. Measures should enable a holistic view to be reached of performance and reduce the likelihood of dysfunctional behaviour.

ACTIVITY **4.2**

Specifying outcomes, outputs, measures and indicators

For your service identify or propose:

- *An outcome*
- *An output*
- *One performance measure*
- *One performance indicator*

Performance improvement

Increased demand for services, raised citizen expectations and significantly diminished resources means achieving high and improving levels of performance is essential for public service leaders.

A major aim of performance management, therefore, should be organisational learning that results in action to improve performance. *The Manager's Guide to Performance Management* (2006: 8) advanced a cycle of plan-do-review-revise which should lead to improvement. The process starts with prioritising and planning performance improvement which is then actioned. The outcomes of the improvement action are reviewed to understand what has worked well/less well, leading to learning and revision in relation to current and future operations as shown in Figure 4.4.

Advances in technology, better understanding of stakeholder needs and what works, together with organisational learning and potential economies of scale means there is usually scope for performance improvement.

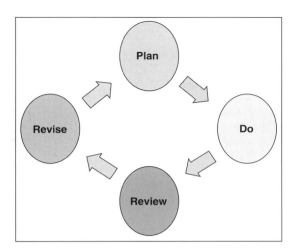

Figure 4.4 Plan-do-review-revise cycle

Performance improvement can involve:

- continuous or adaptive change whereby relatively small improvements result from limited adjustments to how a service is delivered; or
- step change or innovation through making significant or radical change to the features, design and delivery of the service.

The size of the financial challenge facing public sector organisations and environmental factors such as the ageing population require significant step change. This is more likely where:

- the need for step change is widely recognised;
- the culture or 'way things are done round here' encourages innovation or risk taking etc.;
- those involved either have a natural capacity for innovation or possess learned skills. Dr Michael Kirton's adaptor innovator theory (2003) shows that people vary as to whether they tend to think and work largely within the existing paradigm (e.g. adapting services or methods of operating) or they tend to think outside the paradigm (e.g. innovating new services or ways of operating). Irrespective of tendency, managers can develop their capacity to think and act both adaptively and innovatively through using creativity techniques.

Another way of looking at performance improvement is the extent to which it is culturally embedded. The pressure to perform often creates an acute need to act, normally to reduce expenditure. There is a risk that 'quick action' leads to financial savings at the expense of current and/or future service outcomes, particularly where these are not fully understood, measured or communicated. The need for high performance and continuous improvement should permeate the culture such that the importance of performance improvement is recognised, the assumption of personal responsibility is widespread and there is a constant stream of actions leading to improved performance. While an embedded approach is essential, the need for ad hoc studies is likely to remain and a successful organisation is able to pursue and integrate both.

Performance improvements broadly fall into three main groups, economy, efficiency and effectiveness, as can be seen in Figure 4.5.

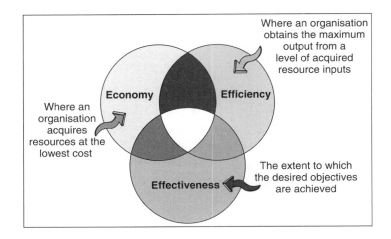

Figure 4.5 Value for money components

Economy improvements include:

- better procurement of buildings, equipment, supplies and services;
- reduced staff costs through pay rate reduction, zero pay awards, decreased pension rights and lowering the organisational level at which tasks are undertaken;
- extending the use of volunteers;
- increasing co-production with service users completing parts of the service previously undertaken by paid staff (e.g. self assessment).

Efficiency improvements include:

- collaborating to share back office services such as financial transaction processing;
- joint senior management teams;
- sharing front office services such as contact centres;
- integrating delivery pathways and joining up responses to 'wicked issues';
- eliminating waste, better storage and transportation of materials and records, better handling of peaks and troughs in demand and well designed layout of premises;
- ensuring error correction is permanent, with action taken to ensure it cannot happen again.

Effectiveness improvements include:

- reviewing service user needs so that services are focused on what is important;
- understanding how pathway activities contribute to the desired outcomes and acting to improve each activity and hand-offs between activities.

Irrespective of whether performance improvement is economic, efficient or effective, care should be taken to look for impact across all three. Sometimes an improvement in one area has negative consequences elsewhere. Purchasing a cheap photocopier, for example, might yield an economic gain but if it keeps jamming this will impact on staff time and paper waste (inefficiency) and possibly lead to poorer copy quality (ineffectiveness). It is also important to recognise the potential longer-term impact of a proposed improvement on other agencies, service users and carers or, more generally, society.

Improving performance

Taking an aspect of your service, identify an improvement you would like to make.

- *What benefits will this improvement yield?*
- *Is the nature of this improvement economy, efficiency or effectiveness?*
- *What needs to change in order for the improvement to happen?*
- *What do you personally need to do?*

Organisational integration

Performance should be integral to the preparation of plans and budgets, business case development, monitoring and review, and staff appraised. A golden thread should link performance objectives from top to bottom so that each employee can see how what they do contributes to the performance of their service, department, organisation and community as shown in Figure 4.6.

The golden thread should also be seen in the way in which roles and responsibilities are allocated and individual performance appraised. Within plans this thread links purpose, outcomes, actions, resources and budgets, thereby ensuring plans and budgets are reconciled and that planned activity is appropriately resourced as shown in Figure 4.7.

Top down or bottom up?

The process by which performance measures are identified and targets set varies on a continuum, at one end of which are organisations where top tier managers determine headline performance objectives which are then specified in increasing detail down the management line; and at the other end, organisations that use a largely bottom up approach where individual services or business units propose performance targets which combine to produce the overall performance objective for the organisation.

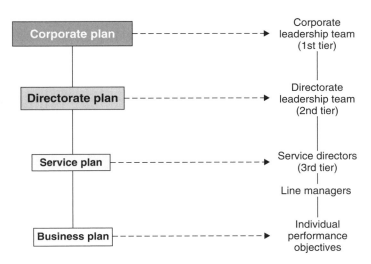

Figure 4.6 Performance as a golden thread

Figure 4.7 Plan golden thread

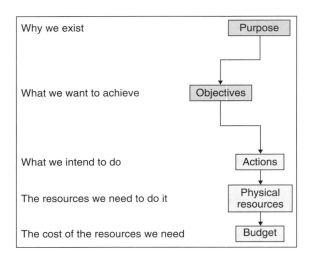

In practice, many organisations adopt a combined approach where, for example, corporate leaders indicate broad performance expectations that more subordinate planners take into account when proposing targets. At the heart of this approach is negotiation and the agreement of targets that are relevant, holistic, challenging and achievable.

Bernard Marr (2009: 137) suggests three main reasons for measuring performance, these being to:

- control behaviour in order to improve conformity and eliminate variance;
- externally report in order to provide information as required by regulation or on a voluntary basis;
- learn and empower employees so that they can make improvement decisions.

Marr presents his reasons for measuring performance diagrammatically as shown in Figure 4.8. Organisations that pursue control and/or external reporting more than learning and empowerment run the risk of counter-productive or dysfunctional behaviour where, for example, individuals act to achieve a performance target even where this is not in the best interests of a service user or, perhaps, overall performance. Where organisations manage in ways where learning and empowerment are pursued more than control and reporting, performance improvements are more likely. Figure 4.9 describes a sequence for performance management.

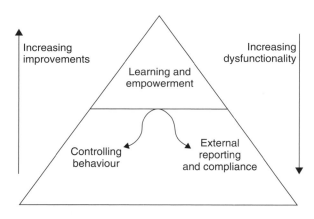

Figure 4.8 Performance management approaches

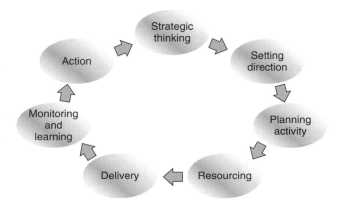

Figure 4.9 Performance planning and action

The process starts with strategic thinking which informs direction setting and forms the basis for detailed activity planning. The next stage is to prepare resource estimates and budgets, following which delivery starts, accompanied by regular monitoring. The primary aim of monitoring should be learning about what is working, what is not working and why so that action can be taken this year and future planning and decision making improved.

ACTIVITY **4.4**

Understanding the performance management process

Through discussion with your line manager discover/confirm the performance management process in the part of the organisation in which you work.

- *What is the process?*
- *How frequently is performance monitored in your part of the organisation?*
- *Who is involved in performance monitoring?*

Developing and using performance measures

If performance management is integral to other organisational processes, identifying measures and setting targets will form part of service planning. Performance measures originate from three main sources: nationally determined, organisationally required, and locally identified. Given the shift towards locally determined performance management, it is likely that fewer of the measures will be set nationally and more locally.

The process (outlined in Figure 4.10) starts with identifying national and organisation-specific performance requirements set by senior managers, trustees, elected members, directors, and so on. National and organisational performance requirements do not necessarily provide a holistic view of performance, so it may be necessary to include locally determined measures. Step 1 involves identifying any performance measures set at a national level that apply to the service or activity in question. Organisational performance requirements are then identified before attention turns to the possible need for local measures. Local measures are identified as part of the direction stage of planning, which starts with the identification of purpose together with key outcomes and objectives.

*Figure 4.10
Setting
performance
measures and
indicators*

1. Identify national performance measures

2. Identify organisational measures

   3. Develop local measures

      a) Confirm purpose

         b) Identify and quantify key outcomes and objectives

           c) Identify measures where possible

              d) Identify indicators where measurement is not possible

                e) Set stretch targets by reference to stakeholder
                   expectations, prior, current and competitor performance

          4. Determine data to gather, analyse
           report and act upon

Once performance measures or indicators are identified, stretch targets are attached that are challenging yet realistic and take account of, for example, stakeholder expectations and prior and current performance. The final stage is to identify the information needed to monitor the measures and indicators so that these can be brought into the wider performance management system.

Importance of performance leadership

Appropriate frameworks, an effective planning system, golden threads, well designed performance measures, rigorous monitoring and control systems are features of an effective approach to performance management. As discussed earlier, effective performance management requires attendance to both hard and soft aspects as defined by the I&DeA and illustrated in Figure 4.11. Undertaken with a focus on hard aspects alone, performance management is likely to be transactional with a reliance on exception reporting, coercion and reward. This is unlikely to result in high performance, especially in times of considerable uncertainty.

High levels of performance and continuous improvement are more likely where the soft aspects are also addressed, in particular, leadership. Performance leadership concerns the 'how' of performance, which, if done well, will result in high levels of motivation, discretionary effort and action. Taking a transformational leadership perspective, Avolio and Bass (2002: 2) identify four components that should be present: *idealised leadership*, where the leader behaves as a role model, *inspirational motivation*, where the leader provides meaning and challenge through shared vision and commitment to goals, *intellectual stimulation*, involving the leader questioning assumptions and encouraging creativity, and *individualised consideration*, where the leader attends to the needs of each individual.

Unless performance leadership is dispersed, there is a risk that with the loss of one charismatic leader, performance will slip. High and improving levels of performance over a sustained period of time are more likely where there is a sound approach to performance management, coupled with a transformational leadership style practised throughout the organisation.

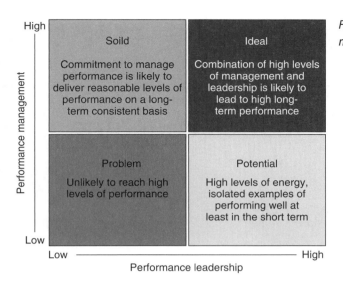

Figure 4.11 Performance management and leadership

TIPS FOR SUCCESS

Managing performance is an important aspect of organisational life which is easy to get wrong. These tips should help you gain the most from this process.

- *Use a range of measures that is sufficiently holistic to get a balanced view of performance.*
- *Ensure selected measures are important to performance.*
- *Take account of measures that are important to other stakeholders, including those set at national and organisational levels.*
- *Take account of the contribution of partners and other agencies.*
- *Be aware of the potential for dysfunctional behaviour and act to reduce or eliminate it.*
- *When comparing performance:*
  - *over time, take into account the effect of factors such as inflation;*
  - *against other services, units or organisations, ensure that comparator organisations are sufficiently similar to make comparison valid;*
  - *against plans, ensure the targets are sufficiently challenging and realistic.*
- *Assess the potential risk that those responsible for performance might focus on achieving personal or team targets to the detriment of the wider purpose.*
- *Identify and take into account variations in performance due to seasonal factors, patterns of demand and other factors outside the control of those leading.*
- *Be aware of potential time lags between taking action and the impact becoming evident.*

Section 5

Introduction to performance coaching

Coaching is arguably the most powerful method for developing managers' capacity for leadership.

(Lee, 2007: 7)

This section introduces a brief history of coaching, defines the term, examines associated concepts, the benefits, and discusses the coaching process in detail. After reading this section, you will be able to undertake a coaching session.

A brief history of coaching

The use of coaching as a development process has increased significantly in recent years, particularly as a tool of choice for improving performance. Despite the obvious use of the word 'coach' in the 1500s as a method of carriage the term was reported to have been adopted in England in the mid-1830s to refer to an individual who assisted students in exam preparation (Zeus and Skiffington, 2005).

From the late 1880s coaching was used in the context of sports, and according to Whitmore (2010: 10), Timothy Gallwey (1974), an educationalist and tennis expert, was the first person in his book *The Inner Game of Tennis* to refer to the spirit of coaching in terms of achieving peak performance, suggesting that 'the opponent within one's own head is more formidable than the one on the other side of the net'.

Sir John Whitmore was a motor racing champion whose book, the renowned *Coaching for Performance*, was published in 1992 and introduced the famous GROW model. Dattner (2007: 3) describes the 1980s as a period when executive coaching 'blossomed and matured' and indeed, in 2005, the Chartered Institute of Personnel and Development (CIPD) described coaching as experiencing an 'explosive growth' and was 'a trend rather than a passing fashion' (CIPD, 2005: 3). Furthermore, figures reported by CIPD in 2006 showed that 80 per cent of all respondents in their survey were investing in coaching; a figure reported to have increased in 2009 to 90 per cent (2009a: 2). This has led to the suggestion that coaching is becoming a standard management practice (CIPD, 2009b).

Webb (2006: 2) reports that such popularity has grown out of a compelling case for coaching based upon the following driving forces:

- complexity – the pace, with frequent and significant changes in the workplace;
- information processes – the move to 'flatter organisations' with the resultant matrix and networked flows of information, which require a different skill set;

- just in time – in a 24-hour culture, expectations are often unrealistic;
- corporate governance – increasing demands on leaner cost effective structures which are much more accountable to the public;
- decision making – leaner structures can create managers who are more isolated;
- lifelong learning – the 'demise of jobs for life' ensures that individuals are under pressure to take greater responsibility not only for their professional development, but ensuring it is the right type matched to future requirements.

According to Webb (2006) coaching meets all the above requirements. Coaching is predominantly found in the commercial sector although it is becoming an emergent model of developing individuals within the public sector.

Coaching defined and explored

Whitmore describes coaching as:

unlocking people's potential to maximise their own performance.

(2010: 10)

The CIPD suggests that:

Coaching helps to raise performance and align people and their goals to the organisation, cements learning and skills, and is a powerful agent for culture change and agility.

(2010: 2)

Lee describes 'leadership coaching' more comprehensively as:

Uniquely placed to draw out the individual qualities of managers and to help them to connect their talents productively to the achievement of organisational goals. Whether the goal is to strengthen interpersonal skills, to build team effectiveness, to enhance influence and impact, or to help managers to adapt quickly to a new role, it is through the reflective environment of leadership coaching that individual qualities can be most effectively nurtured.

(2007: 7)

He goes on to describe this as a crucial role of 'authentic leadership' and 'long-term excellent performance' as one of its 'products'.

Flaherty (2010: 3) draws our attention to the importance of coaching and appreciating it 'from the end', implicitly 'if we know what we are intending to accomplish, we can correct ourselves as we go along and be able to evaluate our success at the end'.

The CIPD (2010) reminds us that coaching can occur in all areas of the organisation, from the front line to executive level and Parsloe (1992) suggests that it is more effective when made a formal requirement and part of a person's role. Others, including Hawkins and Smith (2010: 22) add that it is 'results oriented' and a 'practical' process involving 'adult learning' and 'personal development' which creates a 'collaborative partnership' focused on providing clear feedback.

Indeed, within the literature there is a plethora of definitions (see Appendix 1). Furthermore, there are a number of linked terms from life coaching, executive coaching, personal coaching, skills coaching, business coaching, career coaching, corporate coaching and sales coaching to confidence coaching and relationship coaching and many more. In addition, there are also related concepts within self-development, professional growth and career development, for

Table 5.1 Differences between coaching and therapy

Differences between coaching and therapy

Coaching	Therapy
Present and future focused.	Predominantly present and past focused.
More concerned with action and how things can happen.	More introspective and can be more focused on the 'why'.
Organisational change is frequently the emphasis.	Individual acceptance and change is the focus.
There may be a personal aim but the main emphasis is on performance at work.	More focused on personal crises and problems.
Specified focus.	May be a deeper, broader emphasis.
Does not seek to resolve psychological problems.	Can be used to address psychological issues.
Other individuals can be involved.	Other individuals are less likely to be involved.
Improving an individual's performance and effectiveness at work is the main goal.	An understanding of the underlying cause is a focus.
The aim is towards achieving goals or outcomes.	Potential motivation is to resolve or move away from something painful.
A contract with an organisational sponsor may be the approach.	Unlikely for there to be an individual contract with the sponsoring organisation.
Can be delivered in a group format or as a peer relationship.	Is usually a one to one exchange.

Table 5.2 Differences between coaching and mentoring

Differences between coaching and mentoring

Coaching	Mentoring
The coach can be out of the specialist field.	The mentor is an expert within the same field.
The coach is more frequently from outside the organisation.	The mentor is often from the same organisation.
Can be used for any level and type of employee.	Frequently used in developing the professional mentee.
Focused more on questioning and listening.	Is a source of support, advice, direction and information.
Usually used for a specified period.	Can be a long-term arrangement.
Is not usually focused on teaching specific skills.	May be focused on teaching specific skills and sharing accumulative knowledge.
Exploring with questions and concentrating on immediate goals can be the main aim.	Imparting information, opinions and guidance can be the main focus.

Table 5.2 Continued

Differences between coaching and mentoring

Coaching	Mentoring
The coach doesn't need to be more experienced than the coachee, only knowledgeable and skilled in coaching techniques.	A deliberate matching of an individual who is more experienced, and who can impart their knowledge and wisdom, to a less experienced worker ('expert–novice' relationship).
More appreciative line of questioning and listening.	Can be more directive and telling.
Coaching is not typically associated with induction.	Is typically associated with induction or starting new roles.
The coach adopts more of an explorative approach focusing on work goals.	The mentor often shares their own experiences and can act as a personal advocate.

Table 5.3 Differences between coaching and supervision

Differences between coaching and supervision

Coaching	Supervision
Goal orientated.	Process orientated, systematic review.
Not an essential quality assurance process.	Can be an ongoing quality assurance process.
Not linked to organisational governance requirements.	Connected with organisational governance requirements for public services.
Not specifically linked to professional requirements.	Linked to professional obligations and reflecting on professional practice.
Not specifically focused on implementation of professional standards.	Focused on ensuring service follows best standards, a safe framework of practice.
More focused on a process of inquiry.	Teaching, supporting, facilitating and conceptualising about professional issues and practice.
There is a more accepted mutual relationship.	There is a mutual obligation within the supervision process.
The coach creates solutions with the coachee rather than telling the individual.	The supervisor may tell the supervisee what to do.
The coach may not be more experienced in the coachee's field of practice.	Exchange of advice from an experienced practitioner.
The coachee owns the decisions.	In professional practice can have a shared decision-making process linked to the safety and protection of another individual.

example, therapy, mentoring and supervision. In some literature the terms 'mentoring' and 'coaching' are often used together or interchangeably (Megginson and Clutterbuck, 2010). The tables above, however, differentiate between the concepts. Note – the shorter term 'coaching' throughout denotes 'performance coaching'.

A fundamental principle spanning all of the above approaches is to provide challenge within a safe environment.

ACTIVITY 5.1

Forms of conversation

Identify conversations you have experienced over the last month and select from the terms used in Tables 5.1, 5.2 and 5.3 which description is the most appropriate.

Throughout the coaching literature there is mention of 'coaching conversations'. Coaching happens through a conversation but not all conversations are coaching – so a 'coaching conversation' throughout this book will refer to a deliberate discussion focused upon learning and development where one individual assists another to solve a problem and/or identify and achieve their goals or desired outcomes. It is about helping an individual or team of individuals to gain additional insights to ultimately increase their performance.

Why coaching?

Coaching can produce improved performance for individuals, teams and organisations. Below you'll find a list of some of the well-recognised benefits of coaching. Parsloe (1995: 1) eloquently reminds us that many employees and managers find themselves under so much pressure and are unable to implement a 'coaching management style' because they mistakenly believe there is insufficient time, and coaching requires additional effort. Instead, they resort to believing it is better to 'demand, threaten', or do it themselves. But this approach is flawed for, as Parsloe states:

You have to trust your staff if you want them to produce their best performance.

(1995: 1)

According to the International Coach Federation (2008), as a result of coaching, individuals establish superior goals, take more action, make improved decisions and more fully use their innate abilities. McHale (2008) suggests that coaching is 'one of the few organised means of reaching the third level of learning (Kirkpatrick, 1998) at which behavioural transformation occurs'. Whitmore (2010) reports that there are many benefits of coaching; some of these are identified in Table 5.4, classified within self, team and organisational benefits.

According to the CIPD (2004: 3) the main objective for coaching was for personal development (61 per cent) implemented as part of a wider management and leadership development programme (61 per cent). The third main reason provided in this survey, for coaching, was remedial in cases of poor performance 56 per cent. Although there is some clear evidence that coaching is beneficial, the CIPD (2010: 3) suggests that the 'evaluation gap' remains with only 36 per cent of organisations assessing its impact, with the true benefit of coaching not being identified.

Importantly, 'the quality of the coaching relationship is the single most important determinant of success in coaching' (CIPD, 2007: 3).

Table 5.4 The benefits of performance coaching

	Area	Author
Self	Managing time and commitments better. Helping individuals through transition, for example, new role or promotion.	Maher (2001) Pratt (2004)
	Handling difficult conversations with confidence and developing constructive approaches to challenging unhelpful behaviours, for example, negative thinking and limiting beliefs.	Bossons *et al.* (2009)
	Increased self-awareness, enhanced personal impact and effectiveness.	Starr (2011) Pratt (2004)
	Individual effectiveness with a reported increase in return on investment.	Manchester Study (McGovern *et al.*, 2001)
	Coaching is recognised as 'a very tailored and personalised intervention – a deeper form of development' with individual 'ownership of learning'.	CIPD (2005, 2007: 5)
	An increase in confidence and motivation and improved problem-solving skills.	CIPD (2005)
	Reduce stress and improved work/life balance. And 'enhance the tolerance of complexity' allowing 'wisdom-based decision-making processes'.	Pratt (2004) Webb (2006: 4)
	It is an effective form of continuing professional development.	Lofthouse *et al.* (2010)
Team	'Get your team excited, motivated and engaged at work'.	
	Improved relationships with direct reports (77%). Improved relationships with stakeholders (71%). Improved relationships with peers (61%).	Manchester Study (McGovern *et al.*, 2001: 7)
	Helping teams in transition with change or challenges in short timescales.	CIPD (2007)
	'Decision speed improved especially at senior levels'.	CIPD (2007)
	Encouraging teams to generate more creative and innovative ideas.	Ledgerwood (2003)
	Coaching is infinitely adaptable, inherently personalised and creates a reliable bond, the manager–employee relationship.	BlessingWhite (2008)
	Meets the needs of Generation Y (employees born after 1977), who thrive on feedback.	BlessingWhite (2008)
	Learning collaboratively.	Lofthouse *et al.* (2010)

Table 5.4 Continued

	Area	Author
Organisation	Developing leaders with a strategic capability who can create commitment in teams and individuals without micromanaging them. Individuals managing better in 'flatter organisations'.	Maher (2001)
	Most effective 'talent management' activity.	CIPD (2009b)
	Increased productivity (return on investment was 5.7 times the initial investment), although 73% of the sample identified that the 'value of coaching was either considerably greater or far greater than the money and time invested'.	Manchester Study (McGovern *et al.*, 2001: 6)
	The coaching process allows for more experimental interventions that can be easily evaluated through working with the coach.	CIPD (2007)
	Behavioural change – 'increased proactivity and capacity for addressing issues and more effective management of challenging people'. Higher commitment and more focus on action.	CIPD (2005: 14)
	Increased commitment, satisfaction and retention of staff.	Pratt (2004)
	An effective way of creating learning within an organisation.	CIPD (2004)
	Ensures an organisation can meet the required changes, remain competitive and ensure appropriate succession plans are future proof.	Caplan (2003)

When to coach

Coaching can occur whenever an individual recognises the need and opportunity for it. Potential coachees should know their manager's commitment to coaching and also when, where, and how it will be provided (Parsloe, 1995). Caplan (2003) suggests that it becomes part of an 'every day culture of management and distributed leadership'. Leadership, again, is not about one person.

Megginson and Clutterbuck (2010) also believe peers should coach each other, to exchange experiences and knowledge to increase their level of performance and competence.

Coaching teams as part of the 'manager's day to day activity' is an opportunity, Hardingham *et al.* (2009: 163) believe, 'for people in organisations to become more effective at working and learning together'.

There are lots of opportunities to coach and these arise often when least expected, for example, in corridors, a conversation overheard in the office, a discussion on the phone, someone complaining in a meeting or a conversation with the boss.

Coaching can simply occur when:

someone needs to be able to articulate their thoughts and feelings knowing that they have been listened to, appreciated, taken seriously and can walk away in absolute confidence that their listener thinks no less of them.

(Hardingham *et al.*, 2009: 86)

Section 6
The coaching process

Starting with 'self'

Neill (2009: 2) defines coaching as 'succeeding from the inside out', and believes it should be 'effortless'. Kilburg (2000) describes the coaching process as a 'circle of awareness'. However, the only individual you can truly regulate and manage is you (Patterson *et al.*, 2002).

In essence, as discussed earlier and to be reiterated here, no one can really change how someone does something, only the individual themselves, and as everything we do is based upon thoughts and thinking which invariably creates actions and reactions, the nearest to changing someone's behaviour is by helping them to change their thinking.

To improve someone's performance, therefore, starts with getting the individual to change their thoughts to motivate, if motivation is the issue, or to change their thinking if confidence or self-belief is paralysing them. This comes back to the concept of starting with self before we can begin to create changes in others. Many coaching courses are complemented by psychometric profiling assessments to raise the coach's awareness of self. Becoming more self-aware helps the individual to tune into their own style; their way of thinking, as Neill (2009: 176) describes, to understand their 'unconscious assumptions, filters and habits' and how they impact on others.

Neill (2009) contends that we will almost always see and hear what we are looking for; listening out to confirm our beliefs and assumptions and in so doing delicately creating the world as we perceive it to be. The building blocks of change are fundamentally about developing an awareness of our behaviours and the attributing factors.

Hawkins and Smith (2010) suggest that training programmes for coaches should begin and end with a focus on self-awareness. Increasing self-awareness is about asking good questions and listening – something which will be discussed further in due course.

The famous Johari Window (see Figure 6.1) serves to remind us of the part of ourselves which is not known to us, the part to expand and develop. This cognitive psychology tool, developed in 1955 by Joesph Luft and Harry Ingham, has been used to help people to become more aware and to develop their self-knowledge.

1. Square one is the part of us that is seen by everyone including ourselves – the public view.
2. Square two is what everyone else can see but we cannot and is termed the 'blind spot'.
3. Square three is our private thoughts, things we do not show, but keep to ourselves.
4. Square four represents what no one can see.

This serves to remind us potentially how little we actually know of our 'true selves'. While the so-called window of four panes appears to be equal in size, these would differ depending

Figure 6.1 Johari Window

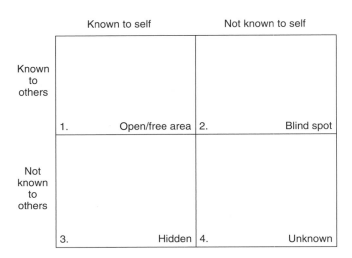

on how much awareness or insight an individual has. Pane one will increase depending on how prepared they are to learn from other people or experiences, and pane two likewise, whether they are prepared to engage with others in self-disclosure.

Developing panes 3 and 4 is about self-discovery, a shared learning process involving others with feedback being one of the primary 'tools'. The fuller Johari Window exercise is detailed in Appendix 2.

The importance of feedback and self-disclosure to learning and development is an integral part of the coaching process.

Key stages

There are key stages or phases within the coaching process; Flaherty (2010: 31) describes these as part of the 'flow' of coaching and non-linear in nature. Sticking to a distinct process whatever that may be, however, is fundamental according to Bossons *et al.* (2009).

> *Relationship remains the beginning point of coaching and its foundation . . . and the basic ingredients for the relationship are mutual trust, respect and freedom of expression.*
>
> (Flaherty, 2010: 33)

O'Neill (2007: 101) has defined four phases to the coaching encounter:

Phase 1 – Contracting

This is described as the 'roots of the coaching phase' and involves establishing the expectations and parameters for the coaching relationship and future encounters. The following are identified as important steps in contracting.

- *Join with the client* — Initial forming of a relationship.
- *Familiarise yourself with the individual's challenge* — Finding out about the issue or problem.
- *Test the individual's ability to own their part of the issue* — Focusing on the coachee's own performance and their 'habitual response to the issue' is the central focus.
- *Give immediate feedback* — This immediacy 'in the moment' provides information about how the individual acts and reacts at work.

• *Take a systems view*	The identified issue is not usually the problem but how the individual manages it within their work environment.
• *Establish a contract*	Is essential for the external and internal coach to ensure there are clear expectations of the coaching sessions and would typically cover the length and frequency of the meetings, managing the agenda, confidentiality, contracts (whether these are legal documents or not), what is written down and who owns this, payment and cancellation terms, what is covered, for example, expenses, venue, contact details, debriefs and follow up sessions with the contractor.
• *Set measurable goals*	and expected outcomes; these should be linked to the required work outcome or result, and are further interlinked with the team and the individual's required behavioural change.
• *Involve the boss*	Coaching should not replace 'in-house performance management', but instead should involve the boss as part of the contract in a three-way meeting, where the boss can articulate their expectations, any monitoring and progress, and agree future meeting schedules as appropriate.

Phase 2 – Planning

• *Move the individual to specifics*	Identify the individual's goals, an action plan and their immediate next steps.
• *Address issues in change management and role clarity*	Help the individual to identify who is the sponsor, the implementer, the decision maker and ask whether people are clear about their roles and responsibilities.
• *Help the individual to identify their side of the pattern*	Their contribution to the issues which now needs to change and any patterns and associated triggers clearly identified.
• *Help the individual plan for resistance.*	Described as inevitable, however, planning can help create realism rather than 'optimism' and identify the individual's own internal resistance.

Phase 3 – Live action coaching

• *Behind the scenes coaching of the individual*	This is spotting the systems at work from the individual's perspective and helping them plan for action.
• *Observation of the coachee in situ*	Observation of the individual provides a whole additional perspective on how they interact and what skills they need to develop.
• *Live action coaching of the coachee and their direct reports in a business meeting*	This is helpful for individuals who are stuck with unproductive patterns in their teams. This 'in the moment' coaching allows debriefing and the team to provide each other with feedback which is non-judgemental (evaluative, e.g. 'you're not listening', 'that was too harsh').

- *Live action coaching of the coachee only, when in business meetings* — This is similar to the above but the only person being coached in this encounter is the coachee. This is real-time coaching.

Phase 4 – Debriefing

- *Evaluation of the individual's effectiveness* — Identifying strengths and challenges, eliciting the individual's thoughts first, celebrating achievements, identifying repeated patterns, and how effective they are at identifying their role, and that of their colleagues. Identifying an ongoing development plan.
- *Evaluation of the coach's effectiveness, including building a mutual feedback loop.* — The individual should be encouraged to provide feedback first; in doing so the coach learns how the coachee provides feedback. The coach reviews and shares how they may have been stuck in the coaching encounter. Revisit the initial contract, outcomes and goals set.

Flaherty (2010: 32) discusses a five-stage approach:

Stage 1 – Establishing a relationship

- *The relationship* — Should be created by being open, appreciative, fair and committed.
- *Coach and coachee* — Should be committed.
- *Mutual trust* — The coach trusts the individual within the coaching encounter, assessing for consistency in what is said and done rather than a universal judgement about the individual.
- *Mutual respect* — Acceptance of the coachee for what they are, and what they present themselves to be. It is not necessary to like someone to coach them and it is important to screen out any prejudices.
- *Mutual freedom of expression* — True freedom of expression exists only when anyone in a conversation can challenge (without fear or negative repercussions) the truth, sincerity, intention and appropriateness of any utterance – coaching is described as a starting place and somewhere to practice. The ability of the coach to really listen and withhold their judgement is important, as is the ability to examine what is true or interesting in what is being said, and be prepared to learn from the encounter.

Stage 2 – Openings

Flaherty talks about individuals living habitual lives of not being sensitive to change, or willing to change and therefore he talks about the coaching 'openings' and describes some of the following as such openings:

- performance reviews;
- broken promises;
- need for a new skill, promotion;
- requests for coaching;
- business needs, for example, greater quality and lower cost;
- project milestones.

Stage 3 – Assessment models

- *Model one: Five elements model* This describes five areas of observation – *immediate concern* (whose immediate concern is it, the coachee or coach?); *commitments* (we are all in the middle of something, what is the coachee committed to?); *future possibilities* (what is the coachee interested in bringing about in the future, what motivates them?); *personal and cultural history* (everyone has had a different experience of life, what is the coachee's?); and *mood* (is the semi-permanent emotional tone within which a person exists, understanding the coachee's mood is therefore important within the coaching encounter).
- *Model two: Domains of competence* The suggestion is to succeed. In anything, an individual must be 'minimally competent' in three areas – *self-management* (we follow through on what we said we would do, and have an appreciation of the effects of our actions on others); *relationships with others* (denotes an individual's 'capacity to develop and maintain long term and mutually satisfying relationships'); and *facts and events* (refers to the capacity to understand processes, systems, models, statistics and mechanisms expertise). Strengths in one domain may be used to cover up weaknesses in another.
- *Model three: Components of satisfaction* This relates to identifying the 'competencies necessary to be both satisfied and effective' and are specific to the area in which the individual is working. These consist of *intellect* ('the ability to predict the future consequences of actions'); *emotion* (the capacity to bring people and events close to us and to distance ourselves from people and events when appropriate'); *will* ('having what we say will happen actually happen'); *context* (creating and maintaining 'meanings, possibilities, actions and relationships that arise once a purpose is declared'); and *soul* ('akin to compassion and kindness, the experience of connectedness to the rest of humanity').

Stage 4 – Enrolment

- *The relationship* (1) Say what could happen in the coaching encounter. (2) The coach declares their commitment to the individual and the possible outcomes. (3) Invites the coachee's commitment. (4) Confronts potential hindrances.

Flaherty suggests that:

> *enrolment demands that we be human; no role or force will fulfil the stage. Manipulation or misrepresentation is quickly shown up. For many potential coaches, managers, teachers and parents, the idea of stepping out of their accustomed roles and positioning themselves as human beings equal to their potential clients is uncomfortable and disconcerting.*

(2010: 107)

Stage 5 – Coaching conversations

- *Type one*   Single conversation to build or improve a competence. It still requires the same foundation of any coaching intervention implicitly – 'the relationship is in place – assessment is completed', an 'opening for coaching has been observed'. Examples would include: 'intervening in aimless complaining, responding to a request about how to do something, and clarifying standards for a presentation'.
- *Type two*   A more complex conversation held over a number of sessions. Examples would include: an individual is not being open to the input of others, the individual is

disorganised, someone is overcommitting themselves, the individual is unassertive.
- *Type three*   A significant and longer conversation is required to create a 'fundamental change'. Examples would include: discovering one's life purpose, beginning or ending a primary relationship, which can include work.

Kilburg (2000) suggests a six-stage coaching process which creates a series of learning loops:

- *Single-loop learning (learning in action)* – Creates greater self-awareness as the individual performs a task or action.
- *Double-loop learning (reflection on learning in action)* – Involves awareness of different ways of completing a task and how to adjust actions in the moment of carrying out the action or task.
- *Triple-loop learning (reflection and further reflection on the learning in action)* – Involves awareness of multiple levels of complexity, polarities and paradoxes in the moment, with the intent of learning how to perform better in the future.

Kilburg describes the stages as follows:

- stage one – establishes containment and typically involves identifying the parameters of the coaching;
- stage two – invites levels of reflection;
- stage three – involves deepening the levels of understanding;
- stage four – involves exploring the choices and options;
- stage five – is an opportunity to implement new behaviours;
- stage six – involves reflecting on and evaluating the outcomes and consequences.

Principles of coaching

The presuppositions or guiding principles which underpin neurolinguistic programming (NLP) could fittingly be applied to coaching. Indeed, Boyes (2006: 18) describes the presuppositions as: 'empowering beliefs for creating change' while Walker (2004: 10) describes them a set of beliefs which 'when acted upon, ensure that communication and change flow in an active dynamic recursive loop'.

Others, for example, Alder (2000) and O'Connor (2001) suggest that they are principles not claimed to be absolute truths, but instead are guiding filters to work with a type of 'instinctive wisdom' (Alder, 2000: 24).

- *The positive worth of the individual is held constant, while the value and appropriateness of internal and/or external behaviour is questioned.*
  People are not broken and don't need to be fixed; their behaviour is useful or not useful and a product of their strategies whether these are useful or not. O'Connor (2001) suggests focusing on changing the strategy to something that is more useful and effective.
- *There is no failure, only feedback – all results and behaviours are achievements, whether they are desired outcomes for a given task/context or not.*
  When you can learn from each mistake, you can see mistakes as feedback, which can be used to improve performance; it is all part of the learning process.

- *The resources an individual needs to effect a change are already within them.*
Everyone has the ability to change their thoughts, feelings, beliefs and behaviours and, therefore, have all the resources to change. The key is how to learn to use these resources to create a permanent change.
- *Underlying all behaviour, there is a positive intention for that individual.*
NLP does not claim that all behaviour is necessarily the best possible choice from an objective point of view, or that it will have positive benefits for everyone; it focuses on separating the intention behind the action from the action or behaviour. As O'Connor (2001: 5) states, 'a person is not their behaviour'.
- *The meaning of the communication is the response you get.*
The success of the communication depends on the communicator. Taking responsibility for your own communication and its effects will provide a much better chance of success than blaming any misunderstandings on those you are communicating with. Furthermore, remember that we are communicating all the time both verbally and non-verbally.
- *Respecting other people's different models of the world creates greater behavioural flexibility.*
This flexibility allows an individual to bridge the gap between their way of thinking and somebody else's and, therefore, enables them to communicate more effectively with that individual.
- *People will normally make the best choices available to them.*
People, within the confines of their current resources, experiences and abilities, will make the best choices they can until they are aware of new options. Creating a greater number of choices and options creates greater flexibility.
- *Everyone has their own unique model (map) of the world.*
Individuals have different past experiences, values and beliefs, which provide them with the so-called 'map of the world'; it is their 'map' and not 'reality' itself; it is a view, a perception, and according to Boyes (2006: 18) by 'changing how you see the world (your map) you will be able to change the results you get in that world'.
- *All information is processed through our senses.*
We make sense of the world through our five senses: we create internal images, hear internal sounds, talk to ourselves, get 'a feeling' for certain things and we interpret tastes and smells in a way that is unique to each of us. This is how we represent the world. Problems are strategies made up from the way we represent the world and, therefore, can be broken down and changed.
- *Mind and body form one system.*
Our thoughts affect our physiology. When we change either, we change the other; changing our thoughts can, therefore, change our behaviour and also our associated physiology.
- *Rapport determines the success in communicating with another person.*
The level of rapport you have with someone will determine the success or otherwise in communicating a specific message.
- *If you want to understand, act.*
You do not really understand something until you have actually done it yourself.

You would add the importance of adhering to agreed-upon confidentiality and that the coach asks the individual to achieve more than they would ask of themselves.

Models of coaching

A model is a strategy or an approach which the coach will follow to achieve a goal or outcome; importantly, the model provides the structure or frame onto which the coaching conversation hangs. According to Lennard (2010):

> a model simplifies and clarifies the complexities of coaching . . . focuses on what is fundamental to coaching . . . and highlights specific elements of coaching.

(2010: 4)

In addition, each model or approach can involve different tools and techniques.

One of the most universally known models within coaching is Whitmore's (2010: 55) GROW model (see Table 6.1) which was originally developed in 1992.

This model is based on a series of open-ended questions, typical of which are those listed in Table 6.2.

The GOAL

Setting a goal for the session is Whitmore's starting point; what does the individual want to achieve within the allocated time? This frames the session and creates clarity of purpose.

The next step he proposes is to identify the coaching goal, stressing the importance of establishing the goal or outcome before it is contaminated by the reality of the situation or

Table 6.1 GROW model

Goal . . .	setting includes the actual session and also for the short, medium and long term.
Reality . . .	checking to explore in full the current situation.
Options . . .	and alternative strategies or courses of action.
Will . . .	what will be done, when, by whom, and the WILL to do it.

Table 6.2 GROW questions

GOAL	What do you want?
	What is the goal for this meeting?
	What does success look like and feel like for you?
	How much influence or control do you have over this goal?
REALITY	What is happening now?
	What have you done so far about this?
	Who is involved and who else could be involved?
	What has stopped you so far from achieving this goal?
OPTIONS	What could you do?
	And what else could you do?
	What are the benefits for each option and are there any costs?
	Can you identify any risks?
WILL	What will you do?
	Will this meet your objective or goal?
	Who needs to know, and what is your next step?
	What support do you need and who will provide this?

past experiences. Focusing on the ideal in this way, he believes, is intrinsically more 'inspiring, creative and motivating'.

He also emphasises the importance of ensuring that the goal identified is in terms of meeting the SMART test:

- Specific
- Measurable
- Agreed
- Relevant/Realistic
- Time bound

But it is also important that the goal is PURE:

- Positively stated
- Understood
- Relevant
- Ethical

And CLEAR:

- Challenging
- Legal
- Environmentally sound
- Appropriate
- Recorded

Whitmore (2010: 59) stresses the importance of identifying not only the 'end goal' but also the 'performance goal'. He defines this as establishing with the coachee the level of performance that is required to achieve the 'end goal'. He suggests that the 'performance goal' is within the coachee's control and, therefore, easier to be responsible and committed to.

The importance of building 'choice' into all aspects of the coaching process is commented on by Whitmore and will be emphasised again within the text.

A common pitfall

A word of caution here is that sometimes, insufficient time is spent identifying the 'real goal' and the temptation to move to the next step of identifying 'the reality' creates a sense of rush or pace within the coaching conversation. If this occurs, looping back should resolve the issue.

Hardingham *et al.* (2009: 103) offer a useful process within this stage to reduce the likelihood of this occurring.

REALITY

Whitmore describes this as identifying what is really happening; assessing the current situation. He believes it will make the goal clearer and identify any potential distortions.

Objective descriptive language is the emphasis at this stage, to encourage the individual to be more specific. Probing for deep awareness is also the motivation and Whitmore states:

We have a measure of choice and control over what we are aware of, but what we are unaware of controls us.

(2010: 70)

Table 6.3 Identifying the real goal

Diagnose	From an examination of what the individual has brought to the session 'articulate a general sense' of what they want to achieve.
Be positive	Check that it is something they want to move towards rather than away from; something to commence doing.
Check commitment	Explore the evidence of how the individual knows they want to achieve the stated aim. Check how the individual knows when they usually want something and establish who they are achieving the stated goal for.
Think systemically	What are the effects of achieving this goal in the broadest sense? How will others react and have they included everyone?
Check control	Explore whether it is within the individual's remit or power to achieve the stated goal. What are the barriers and how could these be overcome?
Assess value	What will be the 'pay off' and is it worth the effort? What might be the consequential outcomes?
Get specific	How will achievement be measured exactly? Could the individual explain it to someone else, and could they clearly understand what will be achieved?
Re-diagnose	Identify whether there has been any change in what they want to achieve – are there other priorities; have sub-goals emerged?
Test reality	Using all of the above information, articulate the goal that now makes sense to the individual.

Source: Hardingham *et al.* (2009: 103)

Encouraging and drawing the individual's attention to what is new, different or what they have missed, is the purpose of this stage. Creating internal awareness increases the likelihood of change; a process Whitmore and others (McDermott and Jago, 2003; Neill, 2009) believe is far more significant when it is from the 'inside' rather than the 'outside'.

Focusing on the reality of the 'emotions' is also a powerful part of this model. Asking how the individual feels can elicit not only the motivation but the deeper thinking behind the emotion. Thoughts implicitly generate emotions, a chemical response within the body (Dispenza, 2007); simplistically changing the thoughts and how an individual is thinking about something will change the reaction and the emotions attached; remembering again that only the individual can change their thinking. Creating a greater awareness and a deeper understanding allows for connections which previously may have not have been apparent (Holroyd, 2012).

Getting the detail of the what, when, who, how and where can reveal some of the objective information that may have been missing or is less obvious. Whitmore would suggest that a thorough exploration at this stage and the goal-setting phase can create an early resolution for the coachee, who may simply have not previously explored the issue in sufficient detail.

A common pitfall
This stage can feel like an interview and can be quite interrogating. It is important, therefore, to use this in an exploratory way, encouraging the individual to talk more than the coach and to explain further.

OPTIONS

The purpose of this phase, according to Whitmore, is to identify all the options rather than the 'right answer' thus maximising the 'choices'.

The question to ask here is: 'What if . . .?'

Whitmore also suggests that each of the options should be examined from a 'benefits and costs' perspective. Encouraging the individual to rank the options provides a natural ordering.

Hardingham *et al.* (2009) talk about the importance of helping the coachee to order things; providing structure in this way, they feel, can reduce the complexity and overwhelming nature of the problem or issue to a more manageable and achievable outcome.

A common pitfall

The coach can fall into the trap of providing the options and selling or emphasising one option more than another. This may come from being more experienced or having faced a similar issue.

Whitmore (2010: 82) suggests that it is appropriate to offer further options once it is clear that the coachee has exhausted their thinking and would not be undermined by the process. He would suggest saying, 'I have another couple of possible options', and 'would you like to hear them?'

WILL

The role of the coach is to help the coachee manage their motivation and involves asking a series of questions, for example:

- What are you going to do?
- What could you do?
- What are you thinking of doing?
- Will this action meet your goal?
- What obstacles might you encounter?
- Who needs to know?
- What support do you need?
- How and when will you elicit this support?
- Rate or rank on a scale of 1–10 the degree of certainty you have in accomplishing the actions?
- What would it need to be a 10?

(Whitmore, 2010: 86–88)

Whitmore would suggest that 'motivation' is the 'holy grail' that every leader would want to find.

A common pitfall

A common pitfall is trying to manage the coachee and 'make them motivated'. This could feel manipulative to the individual rather than spurring them to act. It is for the coachee to manage their own motivation; after all, they are the individual with the action plan. Hardingham *et al.* (2009) would suggest guarding against the following coach motives, 'to help, to connect and to preach'.

See Appendix 3 for examples of GROW questions for each of the four areas.

Establishing a goal

Identify with a colleague a key work goal and, using the GROW model, establish the specific goal and come up with an action plan to achieve the goal.

The debate about models

There are many more models – some are identified in Table 6.4.

Some would argue that the traditional coaching models fail to deliver and that they do not work (Molden, 2010: 26). Molden particularly criticises the GROW model for presuming that the individual is capable of identifying a goal, for he believes coachees are often very 'vague'. Megginson and Clutterbuck (2009) would agree that fixating on a specific goal from the beginning can create too much restriction about the individual and their concerns.

Molden refers to the neurolinguistic programming (NLP) approach to establishing well-formed goals, which moves in the opposite direction from the 'current to the desired state' (see Holroyd, 2012). He argues that any model creates limitations.

Lennard (2010), however, reminds us that the models provide an outline, structure and direction. She also emphasises that models facilitate a method of exploration, which is important to continuous development. Lennard (2010) and Megginson and Clutterbuck (2009) would agree that there is no one recognised approach; they advocate using different models and adapting these to make them personal and resonant.

BlessingWhite (2008: 13) remind us that 'relationships matter most' and would advocate the following key actions, whatever model is used:

1. communicating clearly and candidly;
2. establishing clear performance objectives and milestones;
3. delivering on promises made;
4. recognising the employee's contributions and achievements;
5. taking action to ensure that employees feel important, trusted and valued as a member of the team;
6. being available when employees need advice, information, decisions made or problems solved;
7. respecting the employee's ability to make decisions.

Communication is fundamental to all encounters. Zeus and Skiffington (2001) believe that coaching is fundamentally about questions, not answers. Indeed, Whitmore suggests that:

GROW, without the context of awareness and responsibility and the skill of questioning to generate the goals, has little value.

(2010: 56)

Table 6.4 Other coaching models

Description	Framework	Author
Transformational coaching	1. Listening to the client and system 2. Jointly making sense 3. Generating new options 4. Creating a difference in the room 5. Reflecting on the shift and planning how to embed it NB Practising the 'action stage' in the coaching session, according to the authors, is what makes this model successful.	Hawkins and Smith (2010: 29)
ACE FIRST model of change	**ACTIONS** (what you say or do) **COGNITIONS** (what you think) **EMOTIONS** (what you feel) **FOCUS** (your conscious attention) **INTENTIONS** (your goals) **RESULTS** (the outcomes) **SYSTEM** (the context) **TENSION** (energy in the body) NB According to the author, the above framework is used to describe the individual's experience at a given point in time in relation to a specific context. This is useful to use over time to explore patterns.	Lee (2007: 25)

Table 6.4 Continued

Description	Framework	Author
Transition model	• Starts with a dissatisfaction challenge • Fear and frustration (resolved) • Support commitment responsibility • Action • Transition • Change beliefs • Learning • Change habits NB According to the authors, there is so much to learn once the individual has emerged from the other side of a transition, the most important of which is to change a habit.	O'Connor and Lages (2004: 112)
STEPPPA coaching model	**S:** Subject identified by the coachee **T:** Target objective established and checked **E:** Emotional context to the subject, motivation to change **P:** Perception re-evaluated to create more choice **P:** Plan, a procedure of STEPs leading to the target/goal **P:** Pace, checking the strategy for realism and understanding ramifications of success and failure **A:** Adjust the target strategy or act NB According to the author, this model helps the coach to be sure that the coachee has reached a motivated strategy for success.	McLeod (2009: 189)
The problem-solving sequence	1. Problem identification – what's the problem/challenge? 2. Goal selection – what do I want to achieve? 3. Generation of alternatives – what can I do to achieve my goal? 4. Consideration of the consequences – what are the pros and cons? 5. Decision making – what am I going to do? 6. Implementation – time to do it. NB According to the author, this problem-solving model provides a systematic and structured way of making sure each of the areas are covered.	McMahon (2001: 86)

Section 7

Communication and coaching skills

This section examines three important related communication component elements within the coaching encounter:

- questions;
- listening; and
- non-verbal communication.

  Also included is consideration of the wider set of skills needed for effective coaching.

Questions

O'Connor and Lages (2004: 75) suggest that 'questions are the answers', an emphasis which reflects the importance of questioning within the coaching encounter. According to Bossons *et al.* (2009), questioning 'isn't so much a coaching technique; it is coaching'.

Lee (2007) would agree, describing the significance of 'effective questioning' in guiding the conversation through a 'process of reflection and discovery', identifying the 'challenges and development opportunities' creating insights, clarity and new perspectives and avenues to explore. Whitmore (2010: 44), emphasises raising 'awareness and responsibility' as the primary focus of the coaching question. Such reflection enables an individual to better understand themselves and potentially appreciate why they may have chosen to do some things, and avoid others. Indeed, questions elicit information, can open up an individual's thinking, can expose assumptions, misconceptions, fears, beliefs, values, self-limiting thoughts, strategies and, invariably, can allow a deeper understanding of what matters to the individual and how, through language, they present themselves to the world. Furthermore, all of this information can be challenged through questioning, for example, providing someone with more choices, strategies, a different perspective, to literally see things in a different way.

Questions in the coaching session are primarily about getting the individual to find their own solutions, to think in a different way, to see and own a different perspective and, if appropriate, to behave differently. They are tools to create this opportunity rather than simply telling or instructing. Importantly, within any conversation there is the 'surface structure' of the expressed words, which only reflect part of the 'deeper structure' which is hidden within and is made up of the full details of an experience; thoughts, beliefs, assumptions and, most importantly, the messages that contain all the raw information. (See Holroyd, 2012, for further discussion about this.) Questions are therefore tools to elicit as much of this deeper, raw information to understand and appreciate more fully an individual's reality for them.

Indeed, as McLeod (2009: 7) suggests, questions expose additional information and help the coachee to identify possible 'realities'. He asserts that questioning helps coaching through:

- developing an understanding of the issue and its context;
- exploring historical situations with positive outcomes;
- defining what is, and what is not, in control of the coachee;
- redefining the target(s) and the timescales to success;
- encouraging new perceptions;
- helping the coachee to dissociate from their situation and be more objective;
- re-evaluating value judgements;
- revisiting limiting beliefs;
- recognition of patterns;
- evaluating behaviours in the context of the coachee's identity and values;
- defining the level of certainty the coachee has about their success (motivation).

(McLeod, 2009: 7)

Seeking clarity, facilitating change, creating courage, learning and evaluating progress could all be added to this list.

While Heron's six categories of intervention could be described as a model for understanding interpersonal relationships, the intervention classifications usefully match with the types of questions which can be found in any conversation, whether coaching or otherwise. Heron's six categories of interventions were developed to help therapists (doctors, nurses and counsellors) to identify what therapeutic category of interactions they used and/or preferred. There are two styles identified, 'authoritative' and 'facilitative' which are subdivided into six categories to describe how people intervene when helping.

Hawkins and Smith (2010) suggest that individuals often have a preferred questioning style(s) and to acquire a more versatile appreciation and repertoire to practice developing questions to fit each intervention category. This model can also be used to identify and match the appropriate questions for different categories of problems.

The next question is where to start? Starting with the right motives is critical, together with staying focused (Patterson *et al.*, 2002).

Hardingham *et al.* (2009: 98) would refer to the 'first question' being the most important in building rapport and the one that cannot be prescribed or taken back; it has to fit with the coach and also resonate with the coachee to prevent them from being defensive or forming the wrong first impressions. Megginson and Clutterbuck (2010) suggest starting with the individual; asking about them and what they want. A genuine interest, not a contrived one, is almost too obvious, however, it is important in forging a relationship for, as Flaherty (2010: 39) stresses, 'relationships can't be forced'; instead a 'shared commitment is the basis for a genuine coaching partnership'.

It is important to recognise that in busy organisations some individuals may not be used to answering questions other than those of a superficial nature, or a standard set of the same question format. There is also a degree of courage required to being coached. Creating the right relationship is, therefore, crucial and being able to maintain this requires rapport.

Table 7.1 Heron's six categories

Authoritative	Confronting (confronting)	Be challenging of restrictive attitudes, beliefs and behaviours of others; give direct feedback, for example: Telling someone what you think is holding them back. Playing back what the person has said or done. Helping someone avoid making the same mistake.
	Prescriptive (planning)	Giving advice, telling someone what to do and be directive, for example: 'You need to write a report on that.' 'You need to stand up to your boss.'
	Informative (meaning)	Providing new information, instructing, explaining the background and principles, helping the individual to get a better understanding, for example: 'You will find the same information in this book.' 'This report covers all the facts you will need.'
Facilitative	Supportive (valuing)	Be approving, confirming, validating, praising and show someone that they have your support and commitment, for example: 'I can appreciate how you feel.' 'That must have been very hard for you to endure.'
	Cathartic (feeling)	Releasing tension, encouraging the expression of emotions – laughter, crying; seek to assist the individual to discharge painful emotions, for example: 'What do you really want to say to your boss?'
	Catalytic (structuring)	Ask questions to encourage new thinking, encouraging the individual to generate new options, insights and solutions; be reflective, listen and summarise and then listen some more and encourage self-directed problem solving, for example: 'Can you say any more about that?' 'How could you approach that?' 'If you did know the answer what would it be?'

Source: John Heron (1975), cited by Hawkins and Smith (2010: 131)

Rapport

An important concept within the coaching conversation, McDermott and Jago suggest that:

Rapport comes from showing other people by your behaviour and by your words that you accept the validity of their experience for them. You are meeting them in their model of the world. By so doing you create the basis for cooperative communication . . . Being in rapport is not the same as agreeing with them. You can disagree with someone but still have rapport with them . . . it is the basis for communicating with others.

(2003: 70)

Hardingham *et al.* (2009: 95) describe it as 'mutual recognition and respect' and 'recognition happens as people exchange information about themselves to each other, both explicitly and implicitly'. This approach and commitment allows for deeper understanding and sharing which would not normally occur in everyday conversations. In addition, creating a safe environment for questioning encourages individuals to admit that they 'don't know' – it opens their minds up to learning something new, or a different perspective.

Non-verbal clues

It is important to notice physical reactions, the non-verbal responses within the conversation; for example, facial expressions, tonality, changes in the pitch of the voice, positioning of the body and any other clues that the individual is comfortable with the exchange. If these clues change in response to the questions raised make a note and, if appropriate, draw the individual's attention to the fact. You can do this by building on or changing the question.

Mirroring and matching the individual's voice tone, the pitch, the quality of the voice, the language patterns, the sensory modalities (whether they use visual language, for example, 'I can see it clearly' or auditory, 'I can hear what you are saying'), the tempo and timbre, the breathing and movements or body postures is useful. However, this must be subtle, the timing must be appropriate and with positive regard, otherwise the rapport can be broken if someone believes they are being mimicked.

Questions that create rapport

Being curious about the individual, who they are, what matters to them and how they think are all ways of creating rapport. Being genuine and willing to see things from the coachee's perspective is crucial – take nothing for granted. Affirm the value of someone's comments and thank them for sharing. Revealing your own feelings can help someone feel less exposed. Questions which can create this rapport can be seen in Table 7.2.

Table 7.2 Questions that create rapport

'What is important to you?'	O'Connor and Lages (2004: 81)
Asking questions in relation to the following key personal areas: • their name and its significance to them; • family origin; • home and current family; • education; • work; • successes; • difficulties; • interests; • dreams /aspirations.	Conversational Ladder created by Megginson and Clutterbuck (2010: 19)
'What do you want?'	O'Connor and Lages (2004: 28)
'Could you say more about that?'	Starr (2011)
And simply, 'How can I help?'	

The right questions – great questions

It is not just about what questions to ask but also how to ask them; to be sincere and really curious to learn, rather than to judge or blame. There are a number of different types of question, some of these are detailed in Table 7.3.

Another powerful question which Hardingham *et al.* (2009: 124) would add to the list is a 'differentiating question'; these can be described as encouraging 'reflection' as they cannot be answered without some 'inner mental processing'. The following are cited examples.

- What is the most difficult aspect of your role?
- Who is the best example of that?
- What is the strongest reason for change?

Starting from a broad perspective with open-ended questions, seeking out information and then concentrating increasingly on the detail and the specifics is the questioning process. Before a question is asked, think carefully about the outcome you are trying to achieve.

Asking someone what they feel passionate about is always a good question (Megginson and Clutterbuck, 2010). According to Starr (2011: 89–95) the following are characteristics of 'great' questions:

- *Simple questions* – The coachee doesn't have to spend energy and time trying to work out a 'complex' or clever question.
- *Questions with purpose* – Questions should either be about collecting information or influencing a person's thinking.
- *Influencing without being controlling* – Questions that control can reduce the options, imply judgement or put pressure on someone to say the perceived right answer.

Furthermore, Starr reminds us that, ultimately, the 'best question is one that the coachee is willing to answer'.

'Genuinely exploring unknown territory' and creating new thoughts and insights with skilled questioning is what powerful questions are all about (McDermott and Jago, 2010: 87). They would mention 'inquiry' which is described as an open-ended question, often about values, and provide the following example (2010: 89): 'How would life be different if you weren't

Table 7.3 Types of question

Closed	Closed questions are good for establishing the facts, for example: 'Have I got that right?' (Yes/No)
Open	Open questions require a more descriptive response, and therefore elicit more information, for example: 'What do you want to achieve in your work life?'
Hypothetical	Hypothetical questions explore possibilities and test relationships, and may require a problem-solving approach, for example: 'If all the problems and barriers were removed, how would that change things?'
Leading	Leading questions are assumptive and indirectly hint at how the question should be answered, for example: 'Why do you like being the best?'
Probing	Probing questions are used to gain a deeper appreciation or to identify strategies, for example: 'We've established all the details, now can you tell me how you feel about the situation?'

giving your power away?' This type of question can last beyond the confines of the scheduled session and may be reflected upon and revisited later by the coachee.

Another important type of question is the 'requesting' enquiry, which alerts someone to what is going to happen; such highlighting 'increases active participation' and makes the request a formality while at the same time conveying to the coachee that they have a choice (McDermott and Jago, 2010: 89). The following is an example:

I have a thought I would like to share with you, is that ok? . . . Would you be willing to consider?

(McDermott and Jago, 2010: 90)

Asking permission when it is clear something is difficult is also an important way of respecting the individual; an example of this type of question is:

I sense that you find this topic uncomfortable, but I think it could help to stay with it a little longer. Would you be willing to do that?

(McDermott and Jago, 2010: 91)

O'Connor and Lages (2004: 81) suggest that powerful questions start with the word 'what'. They provide four other key characteristics of powerful coaching questions.

1. Leading to action – solution oriented.
2. Connected to goals rather than problems – moving the client to the future rather than dwelling on the past.
3. Point the way forward – explanations of the past do not necessarily solve problems.
4. Contain powerful assumptions that are helpful, for example: 'What can you learn from this . . . and what will you do differently next time?'

(O'Connor and Lages (2004: 81–82)

'How' questions clearly explore the way that an individual will do something and 'when' questions capture the time.

A note about the WHY question

The 'why' question, which reveals motivation, can be interrogating, creating a defensive stance in the individual who may feel judged. Therefore, the 'why' question is one which some believe should be used sparingly (Whitmore, 2010; O'Connor and Lages, 2004). 'Why' can be replaced by 'what', for example: 'Why did you approach it in that way?' becomes 'What were you trying to do when you approached it in that way'.

Hardingham *et al.* (2009: 132), however, suggest that repeatedly asking the 'why' question can provide a 'deeper and truer understanding of a problem' for it requires deeper analysis and links to reflections about cause and effect.

Neill (2009: 151) suggests that learning about the person's motivation can provide some interesting clues as to whether the individual is governed by what they think they 'should be' or 'should do', rather than what they actually are, or want to do. He suggests listening to see if any of the words in Table 7.4 are used after the 'why' question.

It is not about asking a series of contrived questions, it is about much more.

A cautionary note – leaders mistakenly may feel that they need to have all the answers, solve the problems, provide the information and keep their feelings to themselves; coaching, therefore, may at first feel awkward and counterintuitive.

Table 7.4 Responses to the 'why' question

Want to	Have to	Should
Inner guidance	Means to an end	Self-image
Choice	Prerequisite	The 'right' thing
Inspiration	Desperation	Rationalisation

Source: Neill (2009: 152)

An important combination

'What else . . . and . . . and what else . . . and . . . if there was something else what would that be?' This series of questions is particularly powerful for it really encourages the person to dig deep and, in so doing, come up with either the real thing that is troubling them or an extremely powerful connection, solution or resolution.

This combination links with the next important component of coaching – 'listening', for simply learning a set of great questions is not the way to become a great coach.

Listening

Learn to listen, listen to learn.

(Neill, 2009: 176)

Neill (2009:171) also describes listening as a 'deceptive skill, mostly because it seems as though there's no skill involved at all, but when it comes to our relationships with other people, it is perhaps the most important skill of all'. He suggests that 'we create other people by how we listen to them', listening for evidence to affirm a picture already created in our heads of what the individual's 'persona' represents (2009: 187). Hawkins and Smith (2010) suggest that listening is a skill few of us are schooled in, and fewer of us ever practice. They have developed levels of listening which are outlined in Table 7.5.

Listening is more than just silence; it is about keeping eye contact with supportive gestures of nodding, remaining comfortable in the moment and honouring the silence. Being clear about what you have heard requires clarifying and summarising questions and statements. This allows the coach to assimilate all the facts and provides the coachee with ongoing feedback that they are being listened to carefully, and with respect and consideration for the accuracy of the coachee's story and reflections.

Although Patterson *et al.* (2002) would advocate paraphrasing someone's story as a form of acknowledgement, O'Connor and Lages (2004) argue that it does not show understanding and instead is an interpretation using the coachee's words; invariably the reality for them and therefore risks 'mismatching'. They suggest using the client's own words to check key points of understanding.

We have all experienced the individual who clips the end of our sentences short with words like 'sure' and 'absolutely' or, worse still, completes the sentence. We've also witnessed the individual who looks over your shoulder at the next person they need to talk to, or who is distanced and distracted by the voice in their own head; and when on the phone we've all, at one time or another, heard the keys on the computer being tapped and sense that the

Table 7.5 Levels of listening

Level	Activity of the listener	Outcome registered in the person being listened to
1: Attending	Eye contact and posture demonstrate interest in the other.	'This person wants to listen to me.'
2: Accurate listening	Above, plus accurately paraphrasing what the other is saying.	'This person hears and under-stands what I am talking about.'
3: Empathic listening	Both the above, plus matching their non-verbal cues, sensory frame and metaphors; feeling their situation.	'This person feels what it is like to be in my position, they get my reality.'
4: Generative empathic listening	All the above, plus using one's own intuition and 'felt sense' to connect more fully what one has heard, in the way one plays it back.	'This person helps me to hear myself more fully than I can by myself.'

Source: Hawkins and Smith (2010: 212)

individual we're talking to is not listening. Dattner (2007) recommends that 'good coaching is at least 70% listening'.

Hawkins and Smith (2010: 213) describe the final empathic listening as not only hearing the words but also the 'feelings' and conveying these back to the individual 'verbally and non-verbally', for example, 'It sounds to me as though you are feeling really frustrated with this lack of agreement', matched with the same feelings portrayed by the coachee.

Starr (2011: 75) would point out that the skilled listener can spot a change in the tone of voice; something that denotes the coachee is uncomfortable or that something 'doesn't quite ring true'. She differentiates between 'everyday conversational listening' and the power of 'deep listening' which she suggests creates the sense of the coach being totally focused on the coachee to the point of really sensing who they are. Listening very carefully to the actual words and the language patterns used by the coachee also provides important clues as to what is really happening.

Neill reminds us that:

It's easier to hear what's really going on with other people when we're not trying so hard to listen to them.

(2009: 184)

ACTIVITY **7.1**

Listening

With a colleague, practise simply listening and giving full attention while they talk for three minutes. During this time the only words you can utter are of encouragement, e.g. 'I see', 'Um', etc. Repeat the exercise allowing your colleague to experience being the listener.

Flaherty (2010) suggests that there is more to questions and listening; in the moment, in the space in between, there is a third conversation going on in our heads, adding to the exchange and all of this is almost simultaneous. Neill (2009) suggests the conversation in our heads can stop us really listening to what is being said. This distraction leaks into the exchange with the coachee sensing (unconsciously aware) that the person's presence and attention are missing from the conversation.

Presence and attention

McDermott and Jago (2010) would recommend that these components of coaching conversations are what make the real difference in bringing about change. Flaherty (2010: 101) stresses that 'staying present and attentive' and out of our own heads is part of the natural 'conversation for relationships' he calls 'coaching' – competencies that, he believes, can be learned.

Kline famously uses purposeful silence and listening as a successful technique to encourage and enhance thinking, combined with incisive questions she believes, 'ignites the human mind' (Kline, 2007: 36). McDermott and Jago (2010) agree, suggesting that 'silence well used can enhance the power of almost any question'. They would also stress that silence is 'not a void, it invites, it requires and it invokes'. The essence which it 'invokes' is the 'presence' or being present. Hawkins and Smith (2010) suggest that if we do not develop presence we remain, as Neill (2009) believes, distracted in our thoughts and, therefore, unable to 'fully relate' because we are not fully present.

It is the 'essence of coaching' and lies at its 'core'. McDermott and Jago (2010: 45) believe that 'presence transcends role' and report that, 'in many settings professional expertise is often used as a defensive veneer', instead of being present, which they believe is 'being real'. They make the distinction that 'attention' is about 'noticing, listening and remembering' often using the same words the individual has expressed rather than the coach using their words with their interpretation. Furthermore, they believe this is part of letting someone know that they are 'unique', that they matter, and are respected. Ultimately they describe attention as all about learning to suspend our assumptions.

Paying attention to what 'is' rather than what 'is not', helps individuals to make 'clean connections' with each other rather than become contaminated with assumptions (McDermott and Jago, 2010).

O'Connor and Lages (2004: 72) describe this level of attention as 'conscious listening' where the coach keeps themselves completely out of the way, and believe this is where our 'intuition can work best'.

Intuition

Intuition, according to Starr (2011: 84), is 'wisdom in action', and 'is simply an access to our brain's potential to provide guidance and information free from the confines of our limited conscious mind'. McDermott and Jago (2003: 163) would describe it as our 'gut feelings' and that there is 'always useful information' from the sensation if we choose to act on the feeling.

It is not always clear how to read 'gut feelings' to understand with absolute certainty exactly what the uncomfortable sensation is associated with. Continuing with asking questions from a sense of curiosity and exploration, therefore, will help to reveal the connection. The coach can also simply acknowledge the feeling, for example, 'I feel like there is something missing . . . but don't know what', and see if the coachee can make the connection or elaborate further.

Trust and openness

Trust opens up possibilities that can never exist without it.

(Bossons *et al.*, 2009: 191)

Trust and openness are important components of the coaching relationship. It is connected to the concept of feeling safe, of truth and mutual trust, which is a two-way process. Being open with the coachee and sharing particularly personal information (if this is appropriate), always having the coachee's best interests at heart, acting with integrity, fairness, compassion, respecting their values and being consistent and truthful are the important ingredients which create trust.

Bossons *et al.* (2009: 190) describe the concept of 'self-trust' as crucial in creating trust and advocate that, 'if you don't trust yourself, it's unlikely that others will'. They also suggest that trust is an absolute, an either/or, for there is nothing in between and trust doesn't simply happen 'it requires commitment, personal responsibility and vigilance' (2009: 191). 'Avoiding the power game' for trust is much more durable, flexible and less brittle than power' is the advice Bossons *et al.* (2009: 192) provide.

Flaherty (2010: 41) believes that rather than waiting for trust to be earned over time, it should be given to people like the 'gift' he believes it is. He recognises that in the coaching relationships or conversations, mutual trust can be difficult and advocates finding the 'middle ground' something within which the coach can trust; this may be the consistency of the words used within the exchange. O'Connor and Lages (2004: 11) would advocate being 'real', 'sincere', 'competent', 'honest', 'congruent' and 'present'. Bossons *et al.* would simply say:

We trust them because it's the right thing to do, and in the end, we all benefit by doing the right thing.

(2009: 190)

According to Flaherty, trust links to respect and 'the essence of respect is accepting a person for what they are and what they present themselves to be' (2010: 42).

Putting it together

Spotting both the spoken and the non-verbal clues is a very powerful combination and offers the coach an opportunity to explore further something that may be hidden. It is not just about the words; it is the facial expressions and all the non-verbal body language, the voice quality, tonality, timbre, posture – even the clothes someone wears can create an impression.

Creating a coaching dynamic and using the above techniques is an appropriate and explicitly useful and effective communication approach to use with service users, colleagues, family members and friends.

In summary, putting it together involves:

1. Being ready for coaching
   (i) Being in the right state for coaching ensuring, for example, positive listening and that the internal dialogue is turned down.
   (ii) Creating the right physical environment for rapport –

    a. a neutral place – sometimes away from work can reduce distractions;

    b. no interruptions;

    c. conducive to talking and reflecting, noise levels should be reduced to a minimum;

    d. comfortable, not too cold or too hot, seating and lighting appropriate;

    e. flip charts and notepads may be useful;

    f. refreshments available.

2. Establishing a relationship
   (i) Mutual consent – willingness to participate in coaching.
   (ii) Establishing a development contract with ground rules agreed. This may involve a third party such as the coachee's line manager in a three-way meeting. Depending on the coaching opportunity (for example, a corridor encounter) this can be as simple as asking someone if they would 'like to spend some time talking about' whatever is happening at the time.

3. Creating rapport
   (i) Using all aspects of communication, listening, questioning and non-verbal language.
   (ii) Using presence, attention, trust and your intuition.

4. Goal setting
   (i) Using GROW or any of the other models to identify agreed measurable GOAL(S).

5. Examine the current realities (GROW)
   (i) Establish what is really happening, spend time exploring.

6. Examine the options (GROW)
   (i) and the alternatives considering all the consequences.

7. Establish what the coachee will do (GROW)
   (i) Establish first steps, what next, level of motivation, who else could be, or is, involved and their commitment to action.

8. Agree timescales for review
   (i) These should be explicit and specific.

9. Evaluate and provide feedback
   (i) The feedback can also involve a two-way process.

10. As a coach, ensure that you receive supervision and continuous professional development.

The skills addressed earlier in this section are essential for effective coaching and are a subset of a broader set of skills that are useful when coaching and more generally when exercising leadership.

The CIPD (2004: 36) identified the skills listed in Table 7.6 as characteristics of effective coaches.

Maher (2001) adds the following additional emotional intelligence and behavioural components:

- self-regulation;
- self-motivation;
- accurate empathy;
- social skills.
  Others add the following attitudes:

- self confidence
- transparency
- objectivity

- curiosity
- openness
- balance

- maturity
- self-esteem
- respect

- confidentiality
- organisational awareness
- integrity
- honesty
- positive intent
- continuous learner
- belief in the coachee
- business-mindedness
- flexibility
- goal oriented

(O'Connor and Lages, 2004; Flaherty, 2010; McDermott and Jago, 2010; Lee, 2007; Hardingham *et al.*, 2009)

The coaching competencies identified by the International Coach Federation (2011) include the following:

A. *Setting the foundation*
   1. Meeting ethical guidelines and professional standards
   2. Establishing the coaching agreement
B. *Co-creating the relationship*
   3. Establishing trust and intimacy with the client
   4. Coaching presence
C. *Communicating effectively*
   5. Active listening
   6. Powerful questioning
   7. Direct communication
D. *Facilitating learning and results*
   8. Creating awareness
   9. Designing actions
   10. Planning and goal setting
   11. Managing process and accountability

In addition to these skills, the successful coach has an innate commitment to want to develop and continually learn as a coach and assist other people in doing the same.

Table 7.6 Characteristics of effective coaches

- Self-awareness and self-knowledge
- Clear and effective communication skills (verbal and non-verbal)
- Relationship building skills (including ability to establish rapport)
- Flexibility of approach
- Listening and questioning skills
- Ability to design an effective coaching process
- Ability to assist in goal development and setting, including giving feedback
- Ability to motivate
- Ability to encourage new perspectives
- Ability to assist in making sense of a situation
- Ability to identify significant patterns of thinking and behaving
- Ability to challenge and give feedback
- Ability to establish trust and respect
- Ability to facilitate depth of understanding
- Ability to promote action
- Ability to build resilience

Section 8
Performing organisations

High performing organisations

In Section 4, a high performing organisation was described as one that succeeds in balancing high levels of outcome attainment with high levels of cost effectiveness.

Being either highly cost effective or achieving high levels of outcomes does not constitute high performance, for it is relatively easy to be cost effective if outcome attainment is low, or to achieve higher outcome attainment through using relatively high levels of resource.

The real performance challenge is to deliver high outcomes *and* high cost effectiveness; something which is at the heart of value for money and best value, both of which feature economy, efficiency and effectiveness. Traditionally, effectiveness has been poorly understood and measured, leaving public services exposed to the risk that improvements in economy and efficiency are achieved at the expense of attained outcomes. Overall performance is not improved if all that has occurred is a trade-off between outcomes and cost effectiveness.

The public service value model developed by Cole and Parston (2006: 107) as adapted in Figure 8.1 takes both cost effectiveness and outcome attainment into account, showing how these change over time compared to average performance. An organisation that improves

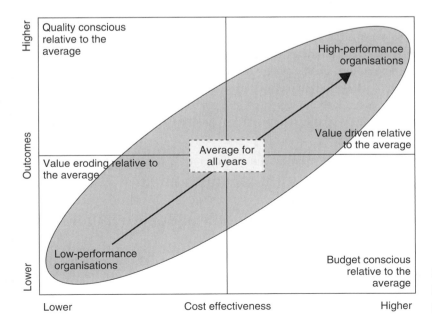

Figure 8.1
Public service
value model

outcomes and cost effectiveness, compared to the average performance over years, will move top right towards high performance. An organisation that improves cost effectiveness but leaves outcomes unaffected will move either towards high performance (where outcome attainment is already high) or budget conscious (where outcome attainment is relatively low).

The government's response to the current recession is pressuring public service leaders to significantly reduce spending, initially through economy and/or efficiency improvement. However, the size of the required reduction is also leading to reduced outcomes in the form of lower service volume and poorer quality.

Another view of high performance is offered by Linda Holbeche (2003: 3–4), author of the *High Performing Checklist*, who suggests that a high performing organisation is one that 'operates on a "both/and" basis – building the foundations for longer-term viability while delivering success in the here and now'. Holbeche identifies that high performing organisations are ones that 'can develop innovative products and services quickly and cost-effectively'; are 'able to operate beyond their own boundaries and maximise potential synergies'; have staff 'who are willing to be flexible and able to deploy their talents to the organisation's advantage'; and are 'customer-focused, aware of the need to respond proactively in a changing marketplace, are able to act responsibly and be accountable for their actions'. In order for this to occur, organisations 'need a culture and management approach which supports and values these behaviours'.

High performance cultures

Embedding high levels of performance and continuous improvement poses a significant organisational design challenge for leaders.

Organisations providing similar public services tend to develop similar statements of purpose, pursue similar outcomes and take similar action. However, such similar organisations may have quite different cultures or 'ways things are done around here'.

Culture is a vital aspect of organisational life and one which some leaders consciously strive to create and maintain. However, this is not true of all leaders, for some appear disinterested or unaware of whether the culture of the organisation they lead is appropriate to the organisational purpose and fits the wider environment. Those who do engage may choose to tailor their own unique culture or adopt a particular unifying theme, for example, a performance culture, learning culture, quality culture or coaching culture.

Johnson *et al*. (2008: 197) present culture as a web at the centre of which is the organisational paradigm, surrounded by elements which combine to deliver the culture.

One way of using the cultural web is to express the paradigm as a recipe for success, as in the following two examples:

We are successful because we maintain an environment in which staff are free to experiment and express themselves.

Or

We are successful because our staff are flexible and can be deployed quickly to meet the changing needs of clients.

These examples imply quite distinct ways of operating, appropriate for some but not all organisations. To be successful an organisational paradigm, or recipe, needs to fit the operating environment for the organisation together with the purpose and objectives, as can be seen in Figure 8.2.

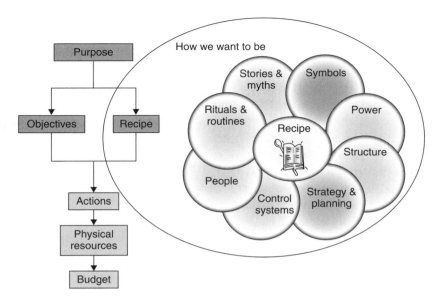

*Figure 8.2
Golden
thread and
recipe*

ACTIVITY **8.1**

Developing a recipe

For your unit, service or organisation, identify the current recipe by completing, in no more than 30 words, the sentence beginning: 'We are successful because . . .'.

The organisational ingredients that make up recipes are many; eight major ones of which can be seen below.

1. The way in which an organisation is organised – for example, the extent to which it is formal or informal, hierarchical or devolved, etc.
2. The types of power used in the organisation, which individuals have power, powerful groupings, forums where decisions are made, etc.
3. How strategy is developed and plans written. The level of detail, flexibility, balance of short and long objectives and the extent to which service user needs drive the process, etc.
4. The ways in which control is exercised, what is controlled and how? How performance is measured, reported, rewarded or punished, etc.
5. How staff are recruited, developed, appraised and rewarded, etc.
6. Day to day acts that explain how things are 'done around here', these tending to highlight what is important in this culture, etc.
7. The stories organisational members tell each other that help explain what is important, how to interpret events, prepare for change and generally behave, etc.
8. Objects, events and acts that have a particular meaning, for example specific words, phrases, acronyms, job titles, uniforms, colour schemes, etc.

Organisational success comes in part from an appropriate recipe accompanied by the correct quantity, quality and mix of ingredients.

A review of the literature reveals that high performing organisations tend to exhibit the cultural characteristics shown in Table 8.1.

Table 8.1 Characteristics of high performing organisations

Characteristics

1. A real commitment to understanding customer need and providing value.
2. Long-lasting relationships are fostered with customers, employees, suppliers etc.
3. Organisational structures are flat and flexible.
4. Staff are encouraged and willing to operate beyond their boundaries.
5. Long- and short-term performance is balanced.
6. There is a focus on continuous improvement.
7. Efficiency action is initiated, not just talked about.
8. Individuals are skilled in problem identification and solution generation.
9. Innovation is quick and effectively implemented.
10. Information is gathered to highlight problems.
11. Knowledge is shared.
12. Reflection is encouraged and learning embraced.
13. Initiative is encouraged amongst staff at every level.
14. Personal responsibility is accepted.
15. Staff enjoy psychological safety – feeling free to try to fail and to learn.

Coaching cultures

Megginson and Clutterbuck define a coaching culture as one where:

> *Coaching is the predominant style of managing and working together, and where a commitment to grow the organisation is embedded in a parallel commitment to grow the people in the organisation.*

(2005: 19)

Megginson and Clutterbuck suggest a typical journey is involved in moving to a coaching culture which has four stages: nascent, tactical, strategic and embedded. Megginson and Clutterbuck also recognise that not all organisational leaders choose to complete the journey to a coaching culture. Similarly, Caplan (2003: 4) recognises the possibility of having a 'culture that is discernibly, though not necessarily exclusively a coaching culture'. Whatever the benefits of coaching, there are a number of reasons for not pursuing a full coaching culture, for example, where it is not appropriate to the environment, senior leaders prefer to focus on a different unifying theme or where it represents too great a shift at present.

Periodically, organisational leaders should explore the extent to which a coaching culture or coaching friendly culture exists by asking the following questions.

1 To what extent do you wish your culture to be coaching friendly (aspiration)?
2. To what extent do you have a coaching friendly culture (reality)?
3. What actions need to be taken to close any gap between aspiration and reality?

Both Caplan (2003) and Megginson and Clutterbuck (2010) suggest ways of assessing the extent to which a coaching culture is present in an organisation. Caplan identifies seven behaviours that she believes are present to some degree in organisations which have to some extent a coaching culture.

1. Everyone in the organisation believes that learning is critical to individual and organisational success.
2. The leaders of the organisation use a non-directive leadership style, that is, they employ a coaching style with peers and subordinates.
3. Decision making is devolved as far as possible to those who are closest to having to implement the decisions.
4. Managers use a coaching style in the way they manage staff on a day-to-day basis.
5. Managers view developing others and creating a learning environment as being one of their major responsibilities.
6. Peers coach one another to share knowledge, to pass on expertise and to help one another, and also raise their own standards and general standards of professionalism.
7. Having a mentor or coach is viewed positively, and people are encouraged to seek mentoring or coaching support at various stages in their career and for various reasons.

(2003: 4)

Megginson and Clutterbuck, taking a broader, more strategic view, measure coaching cultures in terms of the extent to which:

- coaching is linked to business drivers;
- being a coachee is encouraged and supported;
- coach training is provided;
- coaching is rewarded and recognised;
- there is a systemic perspective;
- the move to coaching is managed.

(2005: 97)

While performance and coaching cultures share a number of characteristics, these can differ significantly in practice. The questions contained in Table 8.2 can be used to explore cultures to see the extent to which they have performance and coaching characteristics.

The answers to these questions reveal a picture of the extent to which the culture is likely to deliver high performance and support coaching.

Table 8.2 Cultural web – exploratory questions

Power
 1. How powerful are service users and carers?
 2. To what extent is the prevailing leadership style non-directive?
 3. What is the effect of power on staff motivation, behaviour and relationships?

Structures
 4. Are structures flat or hierarchical, formal or informal?
 5. How devolved is decision making?
 6. Do organisational structures encourage collaboration or competition?
 7. How clear is personal responsibility for performance?
 8. Are staff encouraged to operate beyond their boundaries?
 9. To what extent is upward challenge encouraged?
10. To what extent is coaching formalised, standardised and organised?

Strategy and planning
11. To what extent is customer need understood and value pursued?
12. Are relationships with customers, employees and suppliers long lasting?

Table 8.2 Continued

13. How is planning undertaken and who is involved?
14. Is long- and short-term performance balanced?
15. To what extent are staff proactive?
16. To what extent is continuous improvement pursued?
17. To what extent is innovation stimulated and supported?
18. To what extent is coaching linked to the strategic agenda?

Control systems

19. What gets rewarded?
20. With what frequency is performance monitored?
21. At what level of detail is performance monitored and controlled?
22. What is the main focus for control?
23. How likely is control action to be taken?
24. To what extent is reward and/or punishment linked to control?
25. To what extent is problem and performance information gathered, shared and used?
26. To what extent is effective coaching rewarded?
27. To what extent is coaching used to reveal and share knowledge?

Staffing

28. To what extent is learning and a learning environment encouraged?
29. How are development needs identified?
30. To what extent are staff equipped to problem solve?
31. To what extent is peer to peer, line manager to subordinate and subordinate to line manager coaching practised?
32. To what extent is reflection practised?
33. Which skills are the focus of developmental activity?
34. To what extent is coaching encouraged and supported?
35. What is the process for arranging coaching?
36. To what extent is initiative encouraged?
37. How are coaches recruited, developed and supported?

Rituals and routines

38. Which rituals or routines related to performance are considered important?
39. What role do these rituals and routine play in the success of the organisation?
40. To what extent are meetings a place for listening and learning?
41. What is the frequency and quality of supervision?

Stories and myths

42. What performance stories do people tell?
43. Who are portrayed as performance heroes?
44. What stories are told of those who tried and failed?
45. How widespread are these stories?
46. What beliefs and behaviours do these stories encourage?

Symbols

47. What artefacts, language and metaphor are associated with performance in this organisation?
48. To what extent is coaching viewed positively?
49. To what extent do conversations have a coaching quality?
50. What messages are explicit/implicit in how coaching is promoted within the organisation?

ACTIVITY 8.2

Establishing a goal

- To what extent do you think the culture within your part of your organisation supports high performance and improvement?
- To what extent is the existing culture coaching friendly?
- What ingredient changes would improve your culture (ensuring these are consistent with the recipe developed in Activity 8.1)?

TIPS FOR SUCCESS

- *Performance management involves balancing short- with long-term perspectives and outcome attainment with cost effectiveness.*
- *Current pressure to reduce spending is likely to result in organisations becoming more cost effective with the attendant risk that outcome attainment falls.*
- *A successful organisation has an appropriate recipe coupled with the right quantity, quality and mix of ingredients.*
- *The pursuit of high performance needs to be embedded in the culture.*
- *Organisational leaders should consider the extent to which the culture should be/is 'coaching-friendly'.*
- *The cultural web can be used to clarify the recipe for success, explore the approach to performance management and assess the extent to which the culture is 'coaching-friendly'.*

Section 9
Team coaching

For many people, the ability to work within operational, management or leadership teams is essential to fulfilling their role. By extension, the success of most organisations is dependent on a myriad of teams, each performing at a high level, collaborating with other teams inside and outside the organisation.

When coaching teams, the same skills are required as for one-to-one coaching, coupled with an ability to work in a multi-faceted, dynamic context.

This section identifies key coaching issues relating to team working and offers ideas that can help inform team or group coaching conversations and lead to improved performance.

Groups and teams

The *Collins English Dictionary* defines a group as being:

> *A number of persons or things considered as a collective unit.*

And a team as being:

> *A group of people organised to work together.*

Teams tend to exhibit characteristics such as:

- a sense of shared purpose;
- interaction and interdependence between members;
- frequent communication;
- a sense of belonging;
- a high degree of trust.

Williams (1996: 14) suggests that groups and teams exist on a continuum, at one end of which are groups where members co-exist and at the other end, fully integrated teams. Figure 9.1 shows this continuum.

The collaborative middle ground identified by Williams applies to many management and leadership teams, the members of which do not operate in isolation but at the same time are not as tight knit as operational teams tend to be.

In recent years, the importance of teams has grown, as evidenced by a general movement away from chief officer groups to corporate leadership teams at the highest organisational level. This shift towards teams is in response to a recognised need to move away from organisational silos and to collaborate, the degree, nature and focus of which varies between teams.

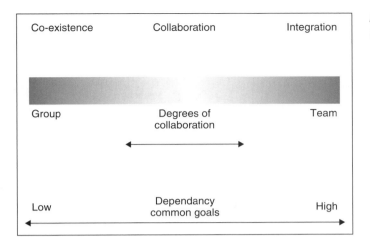

Figure 9.1
Groups and teams

Collaboration may involve one or more of the following:

(i)   sharing information gathering and analysis;
(ii) sharing planning and performance management.;
(iii) working together on cross cutting performance improvement studies;
(iv) individuals representing the team internally and externally;
(v)   networking by individuals on behalf of the team;
(vi) representatives attending conferences and courses and sharing learning.

That leadership and teams have grown in popularity at the same time is no coincidence; for generally, while groups can be managed, teams need to be led.

Team performance

Within public service organisations there are many teams; some of which are linked, some loosely coupled, some operate in isolation and some compete with each other. Leadership teams, management teams, operational teams, project teams and task and finish teams are just some of the types seen within organisations.

The drive to collaborate between agencies and across sectors has created organisational forms such as partnerships, which, while not called teams, have similar processes and require similar skills. Increasingly, individuals are joining together to lead, commission and deliver on behalf, or as part of, a whole community.

While teams differ in their purpose, permanency, membership and size, they share a need to perform, the impact of which can be seen at organisational and community levels.

Katzenbach and Smith (1993: 84) make a link between team effectiveness and performance, identifying four types of team, which they compare with a working group. This is illustrated in Figure 9.2. A working group exists where a number of individuals work in a non-team way, achieving a certain level of performance.

A group of people, mistakenly trying to operate as a team, are likely to perform at a lower level than if they operated as a working group. It is a mistake to think that whenever two or more people work together they have to behave as a team. Forcing a group to be a team wastes time and energy and results in what Katzenbach and Smith refer to as a pseudo team.

Figure 9.2 Team types

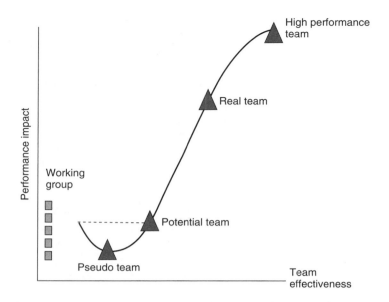

A potential team exists where a collection of individuals have the basics for team building in place. There is significant scope for further development as reflected in the level of performance they achieve.

A real team is defined by Katzenbach and Smith as existing where 'members are equally committed to a common purpose, goals and working approach for which they hold themselves mutually accountable'. Real teams are likely to achieve higher levels of performance than a potential team or if members were to operate as a group. Katzenbach and Smith go on to identify a further level of performance which they label the high performing team and define as 'a real team whose level of commitment to its purpose and goals exceed those of all other like groups and whose members are also committed to one another as individuals'. Often, high performing teams occur where there is a particular challenge, opportunity or crisis.

High performing teams tend to be comparatively rare and short-lived, sharing characteristics such as there being:

- a real belief in the agenda and a drive to achieve;
- high levels of personal commitment;
- high levels of energy and excitement;
- strong accountability;
- less dependency on a formal leader;
- a tendency for members to act and check decisions with the team, rather than the leader;
- high levels of trust;
- a real concern for the development, health and wellbeing of each other;
- a sense of identity and use of humour.

While it might not be possible to create a high performing team, it is possible to coach real teams so that they have the processes, skills and relationships in place to become high performing when needed. The ability to have good quality conversations, seek and receive feedback and to be open to challenge while feeling supported underpins high performing teams.

Team coaching

Team coaching is defined by Clutterbuck as:

Helping the team improve performance, and the process by which performance is achieved through reflection and dialogue.

(2007: 77)

Team coaching is found in four main forms:

1. Where someone from outside the team acts as coach.
2. Where the team leader adopts a coaching style which Clutterbuck (2007: 103–104) considers involves:
   - offering feedback and helping the team question and change its processes;
   - helping the team explore causes of setbacks and failures;
   - improving the team's ability to manage and harness conflict;
   - exploring alignment between personal, sub-team and team goals and encouraging integration of individual and team plans;
   - helping the team engage in reflective dialogue;
   - developing strategy skills, testing the quality of vision and articulating values.
3. Where individual team members make overt or covert coaching contributions.
4. Where the team self-coaches, Clutterbuck (2007: 242) suggests the team:
   - finds the difficult questions, wherever they are;
   - tracks down new knowledge;
   - adapts and leads the coaching process;
   - generates its own feedback, internally and from others;
   - motivates itself to learn.

Team coaching or facilitation?

For a number of years facilitation has been a well-known means by which leadership and organisational development specialists have worked with teams.

Clutterbuck (2007: 101) defines the purpose of facilitation is 'to provide external dialogue management, to help the team reach complex and difficult decisions'. He explains that 'the facilitator is required – like a counsellor or therapist – to maintain a high level of detachment from the issue and to maintain their own focus and that of the team on process. In essence they are catalysts'.

Clutterbuck (2007: 101) considers the purpose of team coaching is 'to empower the team to manage its own dialogue, in order to enhance its capability and performance'. He sees the role of the coach is to 'help the team or an individual create a separate space, where they can collaborate in seeking understanding of the issues. They are engaged with and may be changed by the ensuing dialogue and hence have a role more akin to a reagent.'

In practice there is less clarity between team facilitation and team coaching as approaches to both vary significantly. Some consultants, particularly those with a leadership and management development background have traditionally worked in ways that resemble team coaching and indeed Clutterbuck (2007: 101) makes the point that from time to time 'external coaches in particular may need to adopt a facilitation approach and vice versa'.

69

Coaching and facilitation

Think of a time when you have been part of a team where a meeting, event or project has been led by someone from outside the team.

- *Would you describe their approach as coaching, facilitation, or neither?*
- *What factors influence your view?*

Coaching issues

All team coaching impacts directly or indirectly on performance and this approach should not be limited to 'problem teams' or difficult situations. Groups and pseudo, potential, real and high performing teams can all benefit from coaching conversations.

In practice, however, coaching is often prompted by issues which can be looked at in different ways, including tasks, processes, relationships, meetings and team types.

The task, process and relationships classification shown in Figure 9.3 is a useful way of identifying the focus of coaching activity.

Task issues relate to the strategic and operational responsibilities of the team. For example, an assessment and care management team might engage in coaching conversations regarding assessment practice or how to implement new legislation.

Team process issues include how plans are prepared, meetings conducted and decisions made.

Relationship issues focus on how individuals behave and relate to each other, for example, how well people feel listened to and valued.

Issues often span two or three of these categories which can make them difficult to address, particularly where individuals are experiencing high levels of stress.

Meetings are frequently the focus of coaching and a significant feature of organisational life, including one to one conversations, regular management team meetings, project meetings and away days. Table 9.1 identifies a number of typical issues associated with team meetings, together with implications and potential impact on performance.

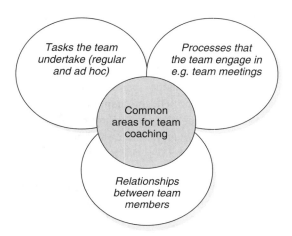

Figure 9.3 Task, process and relationship issues

Table 9.1 Coaching issues – meetings

Potential issues	Implications	Impact on performance
• Lack of focus when addressing an issue, digressions, circular discussions etc. • Decisions that are unravelled after meetings • Lots of noise and energy in meetings but with little progress regarding task • Individuals talked over or excluded, contributions ignored, criticised or rejected • Poor attendance and lateness • Unproductive conflict • Failure to be creative • Individual participants not present for each other – e.g. making phone calls and texting during meetings	• Lengthy meetings • Lack of clarity about whether decisions have been made • Reduced creativity • Slow decision making • Meetings become 'theatre' • Individuals feeling under-valued • Sapped energy • Frustration • Reduced motivation	• Reduced volume of output • Reduced quality of output and impact on outcomes • Poor quality thinking and decision making • Poor staff retention • Lack of capacity to be/ become a high performing team • Personal cost of being a team is high

Having worked with teams over many years, we have seen a number of recurring team types, including *sheltering, nomadic, battling* and *play* teams. These broad types are described in Table 9.2, together with associated coaching areas.

ACTIVITY **9.2**

Team types and issues

Select one of the team types identified in Table 9.2 and assume the role of an external coach. Suggest questions you might use early on in a coaching conversation.

Factors to consider when coaching teams

While coaching teams is similar to coaching individuals, particular care is needed regarding:

Confidentiality

With individual coaching conversations, confidentiality normally involves two people, which might extend to three if the coachee's line manager is involved.

With team coaching, more people are involved and confidentiality extends to the whole team. If coaching sub-groups within a team, there will be layers of confidentiality and unless specific permission is given, what is said in the sub-group should not be shared with the whole team. Similarly, when working with an individual, confidential material should not be shared with the sub-group or whole team.

Table 9.2 *Team types and coaching issues*

Team type and description	Potential coaching areas include
Sheltering Meetings are a refuge from reality. Life is pleasant away from service delivery. Colleagues with similar problems and fears provide mutual support and sympathy. The team feels safe and comfortable and there is much apparent caring for each other. However, there may be some hand-wringing and learned helplessness, tasks may not be tackled and teams often continue beyond useful (task) life.	• Team purpose and the need to exist • Goal setting and monitoring • Team membership • Level of feedback and challenge
Nomadic Discussion wanders all over the place. If there is an agenda it is not observed. Discussions are not finished; decisions are either not reached or not recorded. Team members experience frustration; some might act on their individual understanding of half-agreements.	• Meeting processes • Self-management in preparing for, conduct within and behaviour following meetings • Willingness to challenge focus • Decision making
Battling Team meetings are avoided by some members as these can be a difficult and bad tempered experience. There is significant unproductive conflict sometimes accompanied by verbal bullying and exclusion. Local skirmishes arise from earlier unresolved problems. Less powerful members are cautious about contributing until more powerful members have spoken.	• Conflict management • Basic processes – e.g. contributions in meetings • Listening, questioning and framing contributions
Play When the team meets, members talk a lot but achieve little. Lots of ideas, much enthusiasm, fun and passion. The team meets the needs of those that like to indulge their creative side but can exclude those that feel, or indeed are, less innovative. Playing is often seen to be more enjoyable than sorting out current problems. Difficulty is often experienced with convergent thinking.	• Working with diverse styles and balance • Focus and challenge if necessary • Convergent thinking and action planning • Basic processes – facilitating discussion

Sensitivity

When working with teams, the coach may wish to make contributions that apply to specific members. The coach needs to be sensitive to how members may react to comments made in the presence of other team members. Judgement is needed as to whether specific comments should be made inside or outside the team.

Culture

As with whole organisations, each team within will each have a culture as defined in Section 8. Members develop a way of relating to each other and behaving when working together, sharing stories, metaphors and jokes, knowing which topics can/should not be talked about, etc.

When a new team forms, culture starts to develop from first contact with foundations established during the early stages of team development, then evolving more slowly. Culture may be particularly relevant to the topic being discussed. This can be quite a challenge for an external coach who will need to quickly sense the team culture, be alert to how this might affect conversations and to challenge appropriately. Leader-coaches face a different challenge as they personally influence team culture. Leaders who coach should guard against culture becoming a 'shared given' that limits new ways of looking at things. Related to culture is the idea that teams often have a storyline that plays repeatedly and influences decisions and behaviour. For some teams the storyline becomes 'group think', a phenomenon covered later in this section.

Patterson *et al.* (2002: 21) refer to the importance of having a pool of shared meaning similar to the 'shared understanding' quadrant of the Johari Window introduced in Section 6. With established teams, the coach needs access to this pool which can be gained through careful listening and questioning. With forming teams, the coach may help stimulate the creation or extension of a pool of shared meaning.

Whether external or internal, coaches need to be able to question the existing paradigm or recipe for success, prompt evaluation of individual ingredients and the way these combine.

Relationships within the team

Teams often contain a rich mix of seniority, experience and personal relationships, and 'baggage' associated with prior conflicts, promotion decisions, projects and events.

External coaches usually enter a coaching situation with little understanding of team members as individuals, their history or how they relate to each other. External coaches are not normally in a relationship with, or have prior knowledge of, individual members. This, perhaps, makes it easier for the coach to be objective but leaves them ignorant of potentially important information. The external coach needs to consider whether to seek information about team members prior to coaching, as this can help their preparation but reduce potential objectivity.

Leaders who coach are normally in one-to-one relationships with team members and often privy to sensitive information. Prior relationships, personal knowledge and views held of each other can affect contributions of the leader-coach and team members.

Contracting

As with individual coaching, contracting is an important stage in working with a team.

Team coaching contract

In what respects to you think individual and team coaching contracts differ?

Useful ideas

The following section contains some useful ideas concerning teams that can be a source of insight for the coach and helpful to share with the team. Figure 9.4 identifies six ideas, each of which are developed below.

Figure 9.4
Useful
models – teams

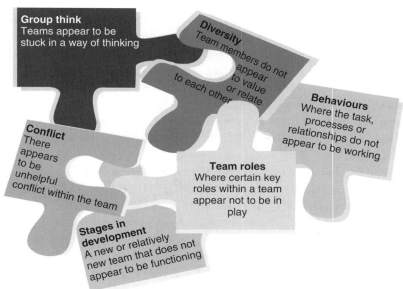

Group think
Teams appear to be stuck in a way of thinking

Diversity
Team members do not appear to value or relate to each other

Behaviours
Where the task, processes or relationships do not appear to be working

Conflict
There appears to be unhelpful conflict within the team

Team roles
Where certain key roles within a team appear not to be in play

Stages in development
A new or relatively new team that does not appear to be functioning

Diversity

In the current environment, teams face considerable challenges, many of which are novel, complex and have a high degree of associated uncertainty. In these situations it is helpful to have diverse teams as these are usually able to tackle a wide range of challenges and engage in productive conflict, resulting in innovation. While different personalities, maps of the world, attitudes to risk, professional backgrounds, age and culture can be highly beneficial to tackling challenges, this diversity can pose a challenge to processes and relationships. In order to gain the full benefit from diversity, it is vital that team members move beyond merely recognising, respecting or even valuing diversity, to harnessing it. This requires each team member to develop the capacity to work with those who they experience as different. As with individual coaching, self-leadership and underpinning emotional intelligence are essential.

Conflict

Contrary to the views and preferences of some individuals, conflict is natural, healthy and potentially productive. The greater the diversity in a team, the greater the potential for conflict, innovation and step change. Taffinder (1998: 124) develops the idea of optimal conflict, illustrated in Figure 9.5, suggesting that this can reduce the likelihood of group think and increase innovation. Conflict arising from different views of how things should be, expressed by passionate individuals within a supportive and encouraging culture, can be extremely beneficial. There are limits, however, to the level of desirable conflict; too little reduces the likelihood of breakthrough thinking, while too much is likely to dampen contributions and lead to wasted energy. Of greater importance, perhaps, than the level of conflict, is the form it takes, of which there are three different types: conflict relating to what needs to be done (task); how it is to be done (process); and how those involved get along (relationships). Relationship and, to a lesser extent, process conflict tend to sap energy, stimulate unhelpful emotional reactions, affect the flow of information and generally distract the team from the task in hand. Task conflict is the most desirable form.

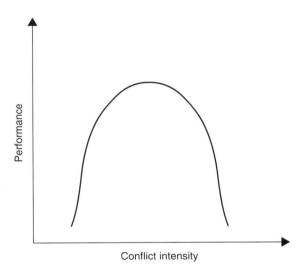

Figure 9.5 Optimal conflict

Stages in development

Mullins (1985: 191), drawing on the work of Tuckman, suggests that newly formed teams follow a fairly predictable development sequence, as illustrated in Figure 9.6. Individuals coming together for the first time spend time forming; understanding their purpose, tentatively getting to know each other and starting to develop processes such as decision making. For many individuals, this stage is typified by caution, time spent sensing what might be going on and establishing their place in the team. Having formed initial relationships, team members start storming as they become aware of different responsibilities, workload and commitment within the team. Caution regarding behaviour is relaxed, some individuals bid for power and there may be early disagreement about tasks, roles and key processes. Assuming successful storming, the group moves into norming where clarity emerges over behaviour, dress, language, humour, etc. Work begins on planning and agreeing standards of performance.

As routines and rituals become clear, the group prepares for the performing stage where norms, relationships and processes are sufficiently established for task completion to become the focus of attention.

Table 9.3 identifies for each stage the typical focus for coaching.

Figure 9.6 Stages in team development

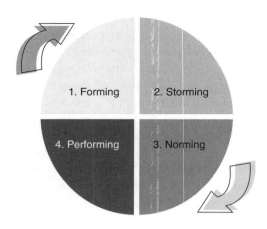

Table 9.3 Stages in development and coaching issues

Stages	Potential coaching focus
Forming	• Creating a productive space • Establishing ground rules • Stimulating learning • Prompting process reviews, reflection and feedback
Storming	• Exploring conflict and prompting productive resolution • Stimulating learning • Challenging and supporting the team to deal with conflict • Prompting process reviews, reflection and feedback
Norming	• Prompting good quality outcomes • Offering observations, voicing the unspoken • Challenging unhelpful behaviour • Stimulating reflection and learning • Prompting process reviews, feedback etc.
Performing	• Stretch-challenging the task • Offering observations and voicing the unspoken • Stimulating learning • Challenging unhelpful behaviour • Prompting process reviews, feedback etc.

Team roles

Belbin (1993) identifies nine roles which an effective team will have access to, balanced in a way that is appropriate to the context. Team roles concern behaviour that is helpful in carrying out functional roles and responsibilities. All roles are of potential value and each has associated allowable weaknesses. However, if these weaknesses are exaggerated they can negatively affect the team; self-awareness and self-management are extremely important. Belbin's (1993: 22) nine team roles are described in Table 9.4.

There is a psychometric instrument that can be completed online (**www.belbin.com**), the output of which can be used to generate insights, stimulate self-awareness and prompt good conversations.

Table 9.4 Belbin's team roles

Role	Description
Plant	Creative, imaginative, unorthodox, solves difficult problems.
Resource investigator	Extrovert, enthusiastic, communicative, explores opportunities, develops contacts.
Coordinator	Mature, confident, good chairperson, clarifies goals, promotes decision making, delegates well.
Shaper	Challenging, dynamic, thrives on pressure, has the drive and courage to overcome obstacles.
Monitor evaluator	Sober, strategic, discerning, sees all options, judges accurately.
Teamworker	Cooperative, mild, perceptive, diplomatic, listens, builds, averts friction, calms the waters.
Implementer	Disciplined, reliable, conservative, efficient, turns ideas into practical actions.
Completer	Painstaking, conscientious, anxious, searches out errors and omissions, delivers on time.
Specialist	Single minded, self-starting, dedicated, provides knowledge and skills in rare supply.

Source: Belbin (1993)

Group think

Occasionally, groups or teams develop a particular and strongly held view of the world. Members insulate themselves from external opinion, protect themselves from information they would prefer not to hear, self-censor doubts or questioning of the shared view, fail to challenge their collective map of the world and discount warnings. As a consequence, team thinking lacks rigour, poor decisions are made and higher than usual levels of risk are taken. Sometimes the group or team, having had previous success, see themselves as winners; invincible, battling against a common external enemy.

When coaching in situations where group think is apparent, the coach can help by asking questions that cause members to:

- explore the idea of individual and collective maps of the world and the potential impact these have on decision making;
- recognise the value of different views and developing a robust thinking process;
- surface questions and concerns;
- bring external views into the conversation.

Coaching situations where group think might be present requires skill to avoid the risk of the coach becoming a 'common enemy'.

Behaviours

Over the years various attempts have been made to classify functions, contributions or behaviours within groups and teams. Mullins (1985: 225) advances the view that 'if the group is to be effective, whatever its structure or the pattern of interrelationships among members, there are two main sets of functions or processes that must be undertaken – task functions and maintenance functions'. Task functions focus on accomplishing the job in hand while maintenance functions build and maintain an effective group or team.

If a team focuses too much on task, at some point they are likely to find processes become difficult and the team unproductive. If the team focuses too much on maintenance, the team can become more like a social or support group with the associated risk that tasks are not completed.

There is a natural tendency to focus on task, particularly when under pressure. Effective leaders and coaches understand this tendency and counter it through deliberate attention to team maintenance or process.

Mullins (1985: 225) cites the work of Benne and Sheats who identify a third type of contribution within groups or teams – self-directed – this being directed towards personal satisfaction.

When coaching, it is useful to look for behaviours associated with these functions or roles, as shown in Figure 9.7. With effective teams, the coach will see a good mix of task and process contributions and little self-directed behaviour.

When observing behaviour, task contributions tend to be easy to spot while process contributions are often quite subtle. Let's take as an example 'gatekeeping', or bringing others into a conversation. A person may demonstrate gatekeeping in an obvious way, saying: 'Let's bring Susan into the conversation at this point' or more naturally: 'Susan what's your take on our position?' A more subtle version would be: 'Does anyone else have any view?' coupled with eye contact and an inviting posture towards Susan.

Self-directed behaviours generally add little to the task or process but satisfy a personal need of the person speaking, for example, to be the centre of attention, gain personal recognition, maintain the status quo, create a crisis, etc. The coach needs to be alert to behaviours that have little task or process impact, for example, sarcasm, name-dropping, idea blocking, conversation domination, showboating and recognition seeking.

It should be noted that many process and self-directed behaviours can be conveyed through posture and facial expression and that individual contributions often combine elements of task and process. Table 9.5 provides examples of common task and process contributions in teams.

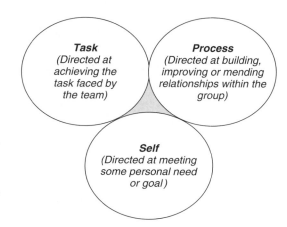

Figure 9.7 Task, process and self-directed behaviour

Table 9.5 Task and process behaviours

Task	Process
Initiating 'Let's start by deciding what we want to achieve today.'	**Encouraging** 'That's great, we have identified a good number of ideas – can anyone think of anything else we might try?'
Seeking information/opinions 'Does anyone know how other services deal with this problem?'	**Gatekeeping** 'John what do you think about whether we should . . .?'
Giving information/opinions 'I think we should move on now.'	**Resolving conflict** 'Let's spend a few minutes exploring these different views.'
Clarifying and elaborating 'Are we looking at this from a client or commissioner perspective?'	**Compromising** 'Having listened to the discussion I may have overstated the benefits of X . . .'
Keeping discussion focused 'So if we could return to the aim of this meeting . . .'	**Following or listening** 'Four of us are broadly in agreement with the proposal and two against. June, can you tell us a little more about your financial reservations?'
Summarising or integrating 'So, we have identified three main advantages for this proposal . . .'	**Standard setting or testing** 'Can I just remind everyone of the ground rules before we start discussions.'
Seeking or taking decisions 'OK, so can we confirm that the aim of this meeting is . . .?'	**Feelings testing** 'I don't know how you are feeling but I am frustrated by our progress so far.'
Evaluating 'It strikes me that there are three minor advantages associated with this option and one significant disadvantage . . .'	**Commenting on team interaction** 'That was a difficult conversation but we reached a good outcome – thankfully we can have a good disagreement without people taking offence.'

ACTIVITY 9.4

Task and process contributions

Next time you are in a meeting, observe contributions.

- *What is the task/process balance of contributions?*
- *Are there any good examples of a task or process contribution?*
- *What feedback would you give to this team?*

Section 10
Coaching and change

Change is the context within which many coaching conversations take place. This section includes examples of change-related topics that often emerge during coaching conversations, addresses the personal impact of change and offers a framework for change and ideas that can lead to potential insights for coaches and coachees.

Definition and types of change

The *Collins Concise Dictionary* defines change as 'to make or become different . . . to transform or convert'.

Currently, significant attention is being paid to transformation where the changes tend to be innovative and deep, impacting on societal or organisational paradigms. As a consequence, individual maps of the world are challenged and redrawn.

Another form of change found more frequently is incremental where adjustments made to systems, roles, frameworks and structures leave the organisational paradigm unchanged. Incremental or adaptive change rarely challenges individual maps of the world and the impact is usually modest and results in continuous improvement.

Individuals tend to be drawn either to transformational or incremental thinking and change. Some people naturally work outside the paradigm, preferring to imagine how things could be different, while others tend to work within the paradigm, adapting current operations and incrementally pursuing efficiency.

The type of change pursued in a situation is influenced by:

- environmental levers for change;
- how organisational 'sense-makers' interpret the scale and nature of the change;
- organisational culture; and
- the balance of influential adaptive and innovative thinkers.

The scale of the present economic situation and the required reduction in public spending cannot be met by conventional small-scale incremental change. The required response will normally involve innovation coupled with a preparedness to be radical, to do things differently or perhaps not at all.

Useful ideas and models

Figure 10.1 identifies six useful ideas concerning change. These ideas can help the coach understand the process they are observing and learning about and might be introduced in conversation with coachees.

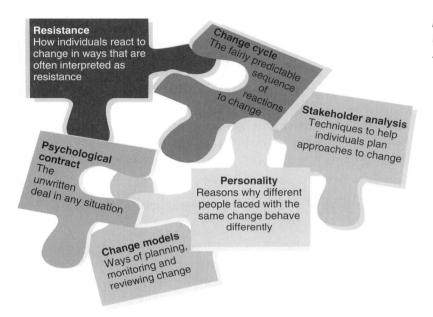

Resistance
How individuals react to change in ways that are often interpreted as resistance

Change cycle
The fairly predictable sequence of reactions to change

Stakeholder analysis
Techniques to help individuals plan approaches to change

Psychological contract
The unwritten deal in any situation

Personality
Reasons why different people faced with the same change behave differently

Change models
Ways of planning, monitoring and reviewing change

Figure 10.1
Useful models
– change

Change cycle

People going through change typically experience a predictable number and sequence of stages. Scott and Jaffe (1989: 35) present this as a grid with individuals moving along a curve from left to right as shown in Figure 10.2.

Two dimensions underpin the diagram: the vertical one, which looks at the extent to which a person is oriented to the outside environment or their inner world, and the horizontal axis, which looks at time. In the denial phase, individuals become aware of the change they face, to which the natural reaction is often numbness and shock followed by denial. Stakeholders can be heard saying things like: 'This will never happen to us', 'We are too good to be affected' or 'We have heard this sort of thing before and nothing ever happens'.

Individuals may not appear affected; performance may remain constant or even increase as people are likely to work harder as they bury their head in the sand.

Over time, denial turns into resistance and the individual becomes more deeply affected, perhaps feeling angry or losing sleep, etc. Individuals might be heard saying things like: 'After all the years of loyalty I have shown, look at how we are being treated' or 'If they think I am going to go along with this they are mistaken'. In time, resistance leads to acceptance that the change will happen and individuals begin exploring what it might mean and what they might need to do. Energy levels tend to pick up but there is still considerable uncertainty and stress. Finally, the experience of exploring the problem, testing new behaviours and developing new skills combine with a better understanding of the change to cause individuals to commit to the new way of being.

Figure 10.2 Change cycle

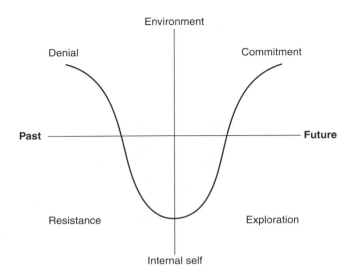

Coaching conversations may take place at any point in the cycle and will, therefore, differ in terms of content, tone and emotion. The coach should be aware that:

- different people may be at different stages on their change journey;
- leaders are likely to be further through the cycle than others;
- the depth and length of the curve is affected by how well the change is led;
- coachees may be experiencing a number of changes at the same time;
- people can move through the early parts of the curve too quickly, particularly if they did not understand the significance of the change;
- performance will vary as individuals go through the curve.

Psychological contract

Employment usually involves a written contract setting out working hours, pay, pension and leave entitlement, etc. An extension of the formal contract is a wider psychological contract based on a 'map of work' accumulated over the years.

Employees bring to their first day in a new post this existing map of work updated for information gained during the recruitment process. This 'anticipated' psychological contract will influence a decision to accept or reject a job offer and shape an individual's expectations of what it will be like working for this employer. This map might include flexibility over work hours, training opportunities, ways of being involved, expectations about coffee breaks, social activities and workload. Over time, the psychological contract for this new post becomes clearer and the map is updated, giving a more accurate sense of what can be expected from an employer and what will be received in return. Similarly, the employer has a view of the psychological contract – a developed sense of how the relationship should be. Changes in a psychological contract often underpin coaching issues and can be a fruitful area to explore, particularly in new employment, promotion or organisational change situations.

Personality

People differ in their experience of and reaction to change, including:

- the extent to which they are tolerant of uncertainty about what might happen, what they should do and actions they might take;
- the extent to which they perceive a change to be risky and whether they seek or avoid risk;
- whether they naturally tend to engage in adaptive or innovative thinking;
- whether they are motivated to avoid things they do not like or are attracted towards outcomes they do like;
- the extent to which they prefer working with the big picture or with detail;
- the level of detail with which they plan.

There are a number of frameworks that can help when exploring reactions to change, including, for example, NLP meta programs, Kirton's Adaptor Innovator theory and the Myers Briggs Type Indicator.

Change models

Over recent years many attempts have been made to identify the steps involved in successful change management.

One popular model is Kotter's (1996: 21) eight steps as shown in Figure 10.3. The first step involves creating a sense of urgency, causing stakeholders to see the need to move away from

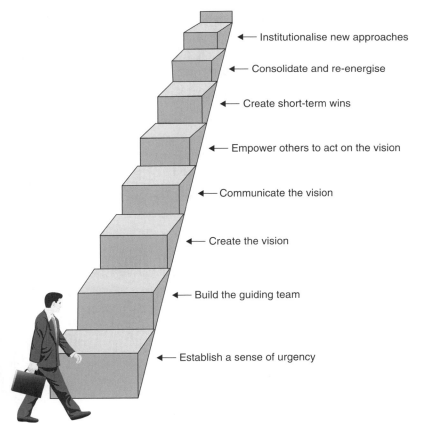

Institutionalise new approaches

Consolidate and re-energise

Create short-term wins

Empower others to act on the vision

Communicate the vision

Create the vision

Build the guiding team

Establish a sense of urgency

Figure 10.3
Kotter's eight
steps model

the current position. Unfavourable comparisons with other organisations, complaints, poor inspection reports, senior leaders sharing their take on the environment and how it is changing are typical ways that an urgency to change can be instilled.

This step is essential to persuading those stakeholders motivated to avoid what they dislike to get behind the change.

The second step is to identify the guiding team – those responsible for designing and implementing this change. This guiding team, or coalition, should extend beyond the formal project group to include stakeholders who are willing and able to guide and champion the change.

The third step is to build a compelling vision, creating a sense of what is to be achieved and what success will look like. A compelling vision motivates stakeholders who are attracted towards what they want.

Having built a compelling vision, the fourth step is to communicate this to different stakeholder groups. Step four involves key messages being repeated many times to ensure the vision is successfully communicated.

Once the vision is known, those responsible for acting need to be empowered; resources made available, obstacles removed and permission given to experiment (step five).

Step six involves maintaining momentum and persuading some of the less resistant stakeholders that the proposed change will happen. It is useful to identify potential quick wins, plan to make these happen and celebrate achievements publicly, rewarding those involved.

To counter the risk of losing focus, momentum and member interest, the seventh step involves consolidating what has happened, rewarding individuals who have been successful and re-energising the change, perhaps with a progress review or a vision refresh. Additions to the guiding team might be made.

The final step is to ensure that the changes made are fixed and that there is no slipping back to how it was before. Rewards are aligned with the new behaviour and other aspects of organisational life (including the planning system and staff appraisals) are amended to reflect the change.

As change is rarely simple, step models can be criticised. In particular, it is often necessary to return to earlier steps and undertake further work. This does not invalidate step models but it does mean they need to be used with care. Kotter's model offers a useful framework for conversations about change and coaches should be alert to common problems such as:

- insufficient time spent on the early steps leading to a failure of preparation;
- failure to properly communicate with those involved in the change;
- insufficient attention given to the last two steps, resulting in change either not being completed or failing to stick.

Kotter's eight steps is a useful framework for exploring a specific change and the coach may be called upon to help individuals or teams use these steps, challenge a current change process or develop a bespoke process.

Stakeholder analysis

Most change situations involve working with a range of stakeholders, some likely to be in favour of the change, others less so. Appreciating stakeholders and their views is important to understanding the change situation, good change design and successful implementation. Four questions are of concern when considering change.

1. Who is affected?
2. What impact might they have on the change process and outcome?
3. What might be behind stakeholder reaction to this change?
4. How might key stakeholders be influenced?

Three techniques can help in developing understanding of stakeholders and an approach to change; a power/interest matrix, force field analysis and attitude analysis. Before using any technique, leaders and coaches should be alert to the risk of labelling as resistant anyone who does not immediately agree with a proposed change. For once identified as resistant, the next step is typically to reduce or counter the influence of those considered resistant. Fullan (2004: 97) makes the point that 'effective leaders in a culture of change appreciate resistance. They reframe it as having possible merit; they almost always deal with it more effectively than anyone else'. Where teams and organisations are diverse, behaviour considered resistant is more likely, healthy and of significant potential value. However, the value of this behaviour is only realised where contributions are channelled in a way that helps develop effective change proposals.

Change leaders need to be able to work with a multitude of stakeholders, including those who:

- have information, perspectives and ideas that will contribute to effective change, e.g. staff;
- can grant or withhold permission or support and may hold resources, e.g. senior management and politicians;
- through their behaviour, will determine whether a change is successful, e.g. staff and service users;
- receive or might receive services, e.g. service users and the wider community;
- pay for services, e.g. local tax payers, service users.

Coaches need to be able to work with a range of individuals involved in change, including those leading, those who are part of a change leadership team, those downstream of change or those concerned on behalf of others, such as service users.

Power/interest matrix
Johnson *et al.* (2008), drawing on earlier models, suggests the use of a power/interest matrix to help identify and sort stakeholders into four main groups, as shown in Figure 10.4. The power

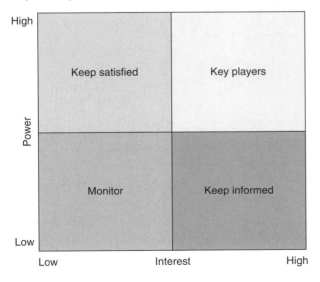

Figure 10.4 Power/interest matrix

dimension concerns the amount of power an individual has in relation to a particular issue, including, for example, granting or withholding permission and resource allocation. The second dimension shows the extent to which stakeholders are likely to show interest in an issue.

Stakeholders with high levels of interest and power are normally key to successful change and great effort needs to be made to engage with them and to satisfy their needs. Those with high power but little interest need to be kept satisfied, at least to avoid the risk that they suddenly become interested in a negative way. Those with high levels of interest but low power might not be able to frustrate change but they may influence others who they could join with to accumulate power. Keeping them informed is important.

Traditionally, those with low levels of power and interest are often considered of little importance. Minimal effort is expended in monitoring to ensure that nothing is changing regarding their level of interest and power. However, in a public service context, these stakeholders merit particular attention for they may include people who are particularly affected by the change but are unlikely to act. This apparent lack of interest, despite impact, can be due to a lack of knowledge, low expectations regarding individual isolation and there being limited channels to voice their interest.

Force field analysis

In any situation prior to change, a number of influences exist in tension. When change is proposed, this status quo will be disturbed; some stakeholders will react favourably, potentially driving the change forward. Those stakeholders that do not perceive this change positively may well resist. This force field can be shown diagrammatically as in Figure 10.5, an example which relates to a workplace in which staff have worked a particular shift pattern for many years.

A manager wishing to change the pattern would quickly find that some people would be in favour, perhaps due to the business argument or new shift times making travel easier for them, for example. Other stakeholders would probably be against this proposal because it might cause problems with childcare arrangements or because they do not like working late in the evening, and so on.

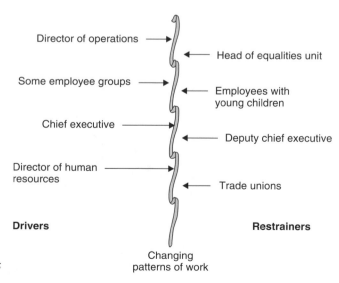

Figure 10.5 *Force field analysis*

Where there are a number of stakeholders, it is useful to understand the shape of the force field; which stakeholders are likely to drive the change, which are relatively neutral and which are likely to resist.

A number of possible benefits flow from force field analysis:

- the planned change might be improved as a result of taking into account new information;
- it might be possible to reduce the degree of resistance;
- strategies for working with resistance can be developed.

When coaching, force field analysis can be useful to map what might be going on in a particular situation and to prompt strategy options. It is also helpful to explore where coachees feature in this force field and why.

The force field can be extended beyond the position of stakeholders to include influences such as systems, resources and capability. The thickness of the lines drawn can be used to denote the perceived significance of stakeholders.

ACTIVITY **10.1**

Force field analysis

In respect of a change you are familiar with, or would like to instigate, prepare a force field diagram.

Attitude analysis

The third mapping tool helpful when coaching is attitude analysis, the source of which is unclear. This framework maps each stakeholder in terms of the perceived current and ideal attitudes to a change as shown in Figure 10.6. Five attitudes are recognised, ranging from resistant on the left and owning on the right. While in an ideal world everyone would buy into, or own, each change this is unlikely in practice. It is not essential that every stakeholder owns a proposed change; for some it is sufficient that they have bought into the change or are simply mildly positive. For others, the best that can be hoped for is that they have a neutral attitude to the proposed change. This framework reveals the attitudinal shift required for each individual and prompts action planning for each individual such as influencing through team briefing, one-to-one conversations and working through a third party.

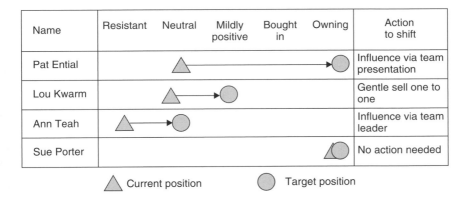

Name	Resistant	Neutral	Mildly positive	Bought in	Owning	Action to shift
Pat Ential						Influence via team presentation
Lou Kwarm						Gentle sell one to one
Ann Teah						Influence via team leader
Sue Porter						No action needed

△ Current position   ◯ Target position

Figure 10.6 Attitude analysis

Resistance

Resistance to a proposed change can be for many reasons and change leaders need to understand which are in play at any point. Reasons for resistance include:

- *psychological* – where individuals react on a personal level linked to varying degrees of need for certainty, different reactions to risk, predispositions towards adaption or innovation, etc.;
- *power* – where the root issue might be a perceived or actual change of status or job title, reduced staff responsibility and/or budget, cessation of membership of management team, loss of promotion prospects, etc.;
- *cognitive* – where the individual disagrees with the change due to perceived flaws in data gathering, analysis, conclusions or suggested actions;
- *value based* – where those affected believe that a proposed change conflicts with one or more values they hold.

If coachees can understand which type of resistance is in play, this can help them develop strategies for working with individuals.

ACTIVITY **10.2**

Cognitive resistance

Faced with a stakeholder who appears to be cognitively resistant, what strategies for working with them might you expect to emerge during a coaching conversation?

Factors to consider when coaching change

There are many factors to consider when coaching change.
Generally it is important to note that:

- the impact of change often goes deeper than simple consideration of what an individual will be doing, who they will be working with or where they will be based;
- individuals experience change within a wider system and this change might coincide with change elsewhere in their lives;
- individual and shared maps of the world influence how change is led and responded to;
- staff and other stakeholders recount stories associated with previous change to help them make sense of what is happening and predict how the change will be handled;
- change may cause other issues to surface for individuals. For example, a change requiring staff to apply for their own posts can rekindle a fear of making presentations. If this fear stops someone from applying for a job the change announcement is likely to have a similar impact as a redundancy notice.

If you are a coach who is also leading the change you:

- will be part of this change, probably further along the change curve and aware of what comes next for the coachee;
- may have information you cannot share;

- may experience similar feelings to the coachee which might make it difficult to help them;
- may in the event of staff redundancy be involved in selecting who stays.

TIPS FOR SUCCESS

- *Be aware of the incremental/transformational nature of change and the extent to which this matches the preferences of those involved in the coaching conversation.*
- *Be aware of maps of the world and the extent to which the psychological contract might be affected by the proposed change.*
- *Be alert to different reactions to change and what might lie behind these.*
- *Be aware of the risk of failing to attend properly to all steps in the change process.*
- *It is important to identify key stakeholders and their attitude to change.*
- *Be aware of the risk of labelling people as resistors, as information they have and views they hold may be critical to success.*

Section 11
Motivation and coaching

This section explores motivation in the context of coaching. Factors that impact on motivation are identified and the importance of language and belief is explored. The section concludes with the identification of factors to take into account when considering motivation.

Achieving emotional commitment for change

Neill reminds us that:

> we are born happy and the worst thing that can ever happen to you is a thought . . . It just means you'll be using what's inside you to create things on the outside, instead of doing them the other way around.

(2009: 2)

The very act of coaching can increase motivation by working in partnership to find solutions, creating a plan, and commitment to achieving the desired outcomes. Neill (2009) focuses on seeing things differently, striving to always be doing something you are totally passionate about, creating a better reality from the inside out.

Feeling motivated at work is inextricably linked to the concept of 'self', personality type, beliefs, values, expectations, previous experiences and what is happening in our personal lives. The important message is to ensure that the roles we choose in life are aligned as much as possible with what intrinsically motivates us.

Aligning goals with an individual's values will enhance their motivation to succeed. For example, if an individual values 'making a difference', linking how a particular goal can make such a difference could be an integral ingredient to achievement.

There are many personal factors which impact upon motivation. McLeod (2009: 142) provides an extensive list of needs (some are detailed below) that he believes are more compelling than wants:

- dynamism;
- working alone;
- working with others;
- positive feedback;
- clear procedures;
- compelling target or goal;
- choices;
- feeling secure.

Two quite straightforward questions everyone should know the answer to in order to improve their productivity in any capacity, at home or work, are:

1. 'When am I most productive?'
2. 'When am I least productive?'

Using this information can help improve the individual's motivation and ability to get important things done when it matters.

Motivations can be mapped and measured over time; one such tool, which is based on Edgar Schein's work, Maslow's hierarchy of needs and the Enneagram, is called 'Motivational Maps' created by James Sale (2011).

Bossons *et al.* (2009: 147) describe eight principles of motivation which they report as originally outlined by John Adair. They believe that these principles should be active at all times rather than used only when someone is sufficiently demotivated. According to the authors, the principles detailed below take into consideration that people are motivated by different things.

Bossons *et al.* remind us that:

motives are inner needs or desires and these can be consciously known to individuals or buried at an unconscious level.

(2009: 148)

They suggest a ninth rule of motivation, 'make clear your intent', and detail the dos and don'ts for coaches relating to sources of motivation (see Appendix 4).

Words that motivate

Molden (2007: 79) discusses the importance of changing from using the word 'that' to 'this'. He argues that an individual creates distance from a task by using the word 'that', for example, 'that project' rather than 'this project'; implicitly, using 'this' creates a greater sense of ownership and with it motivation and commitment. Stephenson (2009: 84) talks about the power and role of 'but' in self-sabotage and describes three types:

'But'

<u>Fear</u>
But what if I fail I will look bad?
But what if I disappoint everyone?

Table 11.1 Eight principles of motivation

Eight principles of motivation
• Be motivated yourself.
• Select people who are highly motivated and matched to the role.
• Treat each person as an individual.
• Set realistic and challenging targets.
• Remember that progress motivates.
• Create an environment that is motivating.
• Provide fair rewards.
• Provide recognition.

But what if I look stupid?
But what if I embarrass myself?

<u>Excuses</u>
But I don't have the time.
But I don't have the energy.
But I am too stressed.
But I am too tired.

<u>Insecurities</u>
But I'm not smart enough.
But I'm not confident enough.

He describes the worst 'but' of all as 'but it is not fair' (p156). Listen for the above and, as a coach, it is useful to mention the connection. Two motivators which fundamentally work in quite opposite ways are described by Rose Charvet (1999: 33) as 'towards' and 'away from' or pleasure versus pain. These concepts are part of a meta-programme of patterns which Rose Charvet advises provide information about what motivates an individual (see also Holroyd, 2012).

To elicit whether someone is motivated by pain or pleasure, ask them what they want in a job, or whatever the situation is, and listen to what they say. Do they mention what they don't want (away from) or what they want (toward)? Two additional factors which are important to consider are whether someone is 'external' or 'internal' (Rose Charvet, 1999: 50).

To elicit this motivation, ask the individual how they know if they have done a good job. An internally-focused person will say that they just know while someone with an external preference will describe what others, such as their boss or their peers, may say.

To elicit this motivational preference, listen to whether the individual provides a lot of detailed information in their responses; invariably specific, or talks in global terms; general, (Rose Charvet, 1997: 96).

Table 11.2 Towards and away factors

Towards (to pleasure)	Away (from pain)
Motivation	**Motivation**
• Focused on their outcome	• Moving away from problems, situations that can cause pain
• Think in terms of goals	• Energised by threats
• What there is to achieve, gain or benefit	• Deadlines and problems to solve
What they say	**What they say**
• Talk about gain, achieve, for example, I would get personal satisfaction and a promotion.	• Talk about issues, problems, risks, for example, there are lots of problems with this report.
Language to motivate them	**Language to motivate them**
• Attain, obtain, get, have, include, achieve, enable, this is what you could accomplish, the benefits of this are, the goal here is to.	• Prevent, avoid, fix, not have to deal with, get rid of, there will be no problems, steer clear of, solve, let's find out what is wrong with it.

The question to elicit this motivational pattern would be to find out how long they have been in a role; if they change jobs frequently, it may suggest that they are motivated by possibilities looking for new experiences.

Molden (2007) would go as far as to say that if a person's role is not aligned with their meta-programme preferences, no amount of threats or praise and encouragement will truly motivate. For example, someone who has to work with detail every day and is motivated by the big picture is going to find it extremely tedious.

Table 11.3 External and internal factors

External (outside criticism)	Internal (self-criticism)
Motivation • They will seek out feedback • Compare their work to others • Outside information is taken as an order or decision	**Motivation** • They evaluate their own performance • They resist being told what to do • They decide • Outside instruction is taken as information
What they say • Am I doing a good job, what do you think to this, I value her opinion as to whether I am cutting it, as an extreme can want constant feedback about their performance.	**What they say** • I know when I have done a good job, I have set my own standards, I don't need any feedback thank you.
Language to motivate them • You'll get good feedback, others will notice, it has been approved by, you will make quite an impact, so and so thinks.	**Language to motivate them** • Only you can decide, you might want to consider, it's up to you, you will know what to do.

Table 11.4 Specific and general factors

Specific (exact/detailed)	General (big picture)
Motivation • Handle small pieces of information well • Like detail • They take in information linear and work step by step	**Motivation** • They can see the end result • Global but can lack detail • Like an overview only
What they say • Lots of detail in their sentences, which may not be required. Every sequence and every action is mentioned.	**What they say** • They can present things in a random order, simple sentences, and brief details only, the basics or a synopsis.
Language to motivate them • Exactly, precisely, detailed, specifically, here are the precise steps, can I give you all the specifics.	**Language to motivate them** • The big picture is, the main idea essentially, the important thing is, in general, basically, in summary.

Table 11.5 Possibility and necessity factors

Possibility	Necessity
Motivation • Motivated by possibilities • Infinite variety of experience • What opportunities might develop • New options, new challenges	**Motivation** • Must do, have to • Accept what is available • What's known and what is secure • More compliant with rules
What they say • What if we try it this way, let's do it differently, this is a new way maybe we could do this? Let's look at all the possibilities. I want.	**What they say** • We must do it this way, these are the rules, and we have to do it like this. We have to follow the plan. I need to, or we need to.
Language to motivate them • New opportunities, new ideas, different ways, different dimensions, should we see what happens?	**Language to motivate them** • You need to, you have to, it is important to, these are the rules and these are the reasons why you must.

The power of beliefs

A belief is just a thought that you've made real.

(Stephenson, 2009: 91)

Stephenson (2009: 92) would further comment that 'a belief has only one job; to gather evidence for its existence'. It is the interpretation of what has occurred rather than what actually happens to an individual. This reiterates the important concept discussed earlier of thoughts producing feelings, emotions and behaviours.

The intensity of a belief and supporting evidence gathered, which can include not only external references but also the influence of internal 'self-talk', determines how an individual feels, thinks and further reinforces the belief. If the belief is productive, as in 'I am succeeding', rather than a limiting belief that 'I will never succeed', the role of belief can be very powerful, particularly in motivating someone to achieve their goals.

Stephenson (2009: 220) suggests that 'learning doesn't occur until a behaviour has changed', i.e. that you can know something on an intellectual or on a logical level but unless you put it into practice and change in some way, you have not truly learned it at all.

Enhancing motivation – additional factors to consider

1. Encouraging an individual to make a public commitment to do something increases motivation.
2. Motivated managers and leaders are more likely to create an atmosphere of reciprocated motivation.
3. Creating a higher aspiration will increase the individual's motivation.

4. Self-rewards creating both physical and mental rewards; the latter is about positive self-talk, for example, praise. Manz *et al.* (1997) would suggest identifying the factors an individual finds rewarding and using these intentionally to increase motivation and effectiveness.

5. Reminding individuals that they have a choice, they can focus on what went well, or dwell on what they perceived to have gone wrong. This links to the concept of what you focus on is what you get.

6. Recognising energy depleting behaviours and committing to changing these by doing something better instead.

7. Ensuring someone feels safe to explore their 'motivation' and identifying what is impacting upon it honestly is crucial in performance coaching and enhancing an individual's motivation.

8. Encourage an individual to own successes by talking in an 'active' rather than 'passive voice', for example, 'I achieved the goal', instead of 'the goal was achieved' (O'Connor and Lages, 2004: 32). Remember, success breeds success.

9. Megginson and Clutterbuck (2009: 195) advise coaches to ask: 'For whose benefit am I asking this question?' to ensure that they are concentrating on the coachee's motivation and not their own.

10. Starting with an immediate issue in a coaching session creates an appreciation that there is an undertaking and, therefore, motivation to find a resolution (O'Connor and Lages, 2004).

11. Treating individuals as unique reminds us that people are motivated by different things. Coaching, after all, provides the medium to discover what an individual's motivators are.

12. Blanchard *et al.* (2006) suggest that 'when your competence is low, you need direction; when your commitment is low you need support'. He details support as helping someone to problem solve by listening, encouraging and sharing.

The special case of Generation Y

BlessingWhite (2009) remind us that people like to coach and be coached. In their international study, 87 per cent of individuals reported that they strongly agreed that, in general, they like to be coached; this is particularly important for Generation 'Y' individuals (BlessingWhite, 2008: 8).

Generation Y-ers are people born from 1977 onwards and, unlike their parents, are similar to the veterans and get on well with the baby boomers. Generation Y individuals, who have been brought up on affection, praise and flattery expect a high degree of feedback and are 'well educated, well-informed, motivated and flexible'. They want managers to coach them and provide informal mentoring (Trotereau, 2008).

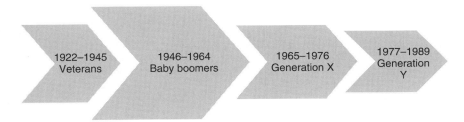

Figure 11.1 Generation timeline

Kelan *et al.* (2009:4) call them the 'reflexive generation' as they are constantly reflecting back on the relationship between 'self, work and life' and, most importantly, require feedback. Kelan *et al.*'s research identified that these individuals found performance management practices to be 'too slow, bureaucratic and too hierarchical'. For this generation, the emphasis is on 'work to learn' rather than 'work to live' (unlike Generation X) and they want a coaching manager who will help them to develop (Kelan *et al.*, 2009). This links with the next important role for the coach: providing feedback.

Section 12
Feedback

This section explains how feedback can assist in coaching, introduces useful ideas and offers guidance on giving and receiving feedback.

Providing effective feedback

Two models can be useful in improving performance and offering feedback. The IGROW model (Table 12.1) can be used for a change in behaviour or to improve performance.

The EEC model is used for providing observed feedback.

Other models, for example BISA, would add a silence and pause after the second 'E' to ensure that the individual can stop to reflect and respond to the information provided:

Behaviour – specific behaviour, the facts.

Impact – the impact of the behaviour on the people present.

Silence – let the individual reflect on the information and respond.

Alternative – ideas for how they could have responded more effectively.

Providing team feedback may include the following questions:

- What worked well?
- What did not work well?
- What could we do differently next time?

Table 12.1 IGROW model

I	Issue	Identifying the performance improvement opportunity, including clearly measurable objectives or outcomes.
G	Goal	Presenting the goal for the coaching conversation, for example, 'I want to explore the difficulties you've previously described. . .'
R	Root cause	Get the coachee to explore and examine their thoughts about the specific difficulties.
O	Options	Creating a plan to address the difficulties is the focus of this stage and should include opportunities for new learning and rehearsal. Additional feedback provided.
W	What's next?	The individual should identify the next actions and tasks in relation to implementing the plan.

Table 12.2 EEC model

E	Example/facts	1. Tell the individual what they did. 2. Provide the facts. 3. Be specific/non-emotional.
E	Effect/impact	1. Describe the effect their action had on you. 2. Share your feelings. 3. Use 'I' statements.
C	Change	1. Encourage the individual to identify changes. 2. Ask them to reflect on what they could have done differently. 3. Encourage them to identify their own changes.

Approaches and strategies that could be adopted include:

- reflecting back;
- being balanced;
- active listening;
- observing body language;
- being tentative;
- maintaining silence;
- being sensitive;
- allowing time for questions;
- being objective;
- having positive regard;
- being curious;
- acting in a timely way;
- being specific;
- summarising events.

Hardingham *et al.* (2009) remind us that the single purpose of providing feedback in the coaching encounter is to help the coachee to achieve their goals. There is no hidden agenda, simply a positive intention to develop a coachee's self-awareness in the present through a reflective process. It is a crucial aspect of the coaching partnership and happens continuously during the whole coaching journey (McDowall, 2008).

Hawkins and Smith (2010: 168) draw our attention to Irving Yalom's (2002) advice; to always attend to what is occurring in the 'here and now' of all professional relationships. He describes 'here' in relation to where something is happening, e.g. in the office, the corridor, the relationship, the discussion or in the space between 'me and you' whereas 'now' refers to the present time.

Hardingham *et al.* (2009: 181) would agree that providing the 'permission-seeking bit of coaching' has been satisfied, 'corridor coaching' can provide some of the most effective and productive feedback opportunities that someone can ever receive. They would suggest that 'corridor coaching' actually fundamentally changes the 'culture of the organisation' and, rather than a formal process of coaching, offers in the moment opportunities to weave change into the tapestry of the organisation (2009: 182). More formal coaching can be used to deal with complex and difficult issues. Hardingham *et al.* also advise that people are always in the middle of something, so to check first whether it is appropriate to coach at that moment.

They recommend that managers who coach should:

1. Make the distinction between coaching and formal performance management when disciplinary action may be part of the process, in which case, human resources should be involved.
2. Ask for permission to coach; if this is not given, don't coach.
3. Do not give advice under the name of coaching, keep curious.
4. Make use of the precious time available; travelling in cars to meetings.
5. Be observant; look for opportunities to help someone to develop further by providing immediate feedback.

(2009: 183)

Hawkins and Smith (2010: 225) described feedback as the 'process of telling another person how they are experienced' and warn that it can be fraught with problems and anxiety because negative feedback can have many past associations, for example, something being wrong and believe this could result in feedback being 'given badly'.

They stress that providing clear feedback, which is not tainted by any hidden agendas, is very powerful, 'a rare gift' to give to someone (p226). This, therefore, requires listening and observing 'cleanly' and then feeding back what was actually experienced (p226). Individuals will always be clear about what is expected of them and feel supported to achieve the very best they can.

McDowall (2008) reminds us that within any task there is feedback from the task itself and this may reinforce that it is challenging, producing perhaps resentment or disappointment in the individual. This together with peers, managers and others creates the complex concept of multiple sources of feedback, which may reveal different information but with a common core. McDowall describes an authoritative figure being listened to and adhered to more. In addition, the message from someone who provides feedback who is perceived as credible and respected is also more likely to be accepted.

Although research seems to suggest that we want feedback, whether an individual actually does something about it can be related to their self-regard and wish to develop (McDowall, 2008).

People with low self-esteem who receive negative feedback are more likely to reduce their commitment to the organisation (McDowall, 2008). McDowall states that 'feedback should be explained clearly and should relate to future oriented targets to ensure that it is relevant to individuals and achieves lasting impact' and, importantly, even if the message is 'positive or negative' it should not matter. Another significant factor is an individual's belief that they can change things – 'self-efficacy'.

Furthermore, the research supports the notion that 'those who perceived more support from their supervisors put more effort into their development and engaged in more development activities' (McDowall, 2008: 35).

For a busy manager, providing ongoing performance feedback and coaching against identified goals will, in the long term, save time. 'Self-belief' is also essential as individuals need to believe that they can change (McDowall, 2008).

BlessingWhite (2008: 7) suggest that managers often worry that they should have 'all the answers' but staff instead want to be 'stretched' and helped to resolve any problems; they 'don't want advice'; they want 'trusting, supportive relationships'.

Giving feedback can say as much about the provider of the feedback as the person receiving it. Hawkins and Smith (2010: 226) use the mnemonic CORBS as a reminder of how to give effective feedback.

Clear	Being clear. Check for understanding from the coachee.
Owned	Use the word 'I', feedback is always the coach's perspective.
	The word 'you' can be perceived as accusative.
Regular	If provided on a regular basis, is more likely to be useful.
	Always give feedback as close to the event as possible, don't store things up.
Balanced	This should be balanced in terms of negative and positive.
	If the feedback is always positive it may suggest that there is some distortion.
Specific	Individuals cannot learn from generalised feedback, it needs to be specific to time and place and objective, factual, quantified and expectations articulated.

Added to this should always be with positive intent and the environment conducive for such conversations, for example, free from interruptions, and the exchange sufficiently long enough to allow for the messages to be reflected upon and discussed. Any stipulated actions should also be captured and appropriate time expectations agreed.

McDowall (2008) summarises that feedback always needs to be clear, linked to personal goals, and goals set should be benchmarked and followed up by the coach to ensure that they are both effective and the learning is transferred to new situations. It is also important that the coach believes that the individual can change.

Table 12.3 Effective and ineffective feedback

Effective feedback	Ineffective feedback
The complexity of feedback is understood by the coach, e.g. that individuals will react differently.	There is no common frame of reference.
There is effective communication and interpersonal rapport between coach and coachee.	No goals, or insufficiently specified goals, have been agreed.
The coach is seen as credible.	The coach lacks credibility.
The coachee is in a receptive state, and has the motivation and ability to do something as a result of the feedback.	The coachee lacks self-esteem and belief that he or she has the power to change.
The feedback message contains clear evidence of behaviours.	There is little support in the environment and from the client.
Feedback is given at the right time, in the right place.	The coach shies away from offering critical feedback.
The coach believes that the coachee can change.	The feedback message is threatening and personal.
The coach is able to adapt his/her feedback style in an appropriate manner.	Feedback is negative and out of the blue.

Source: McDowall (2008: 40)

Celebrating successes, providing positive feedback, whilst on the surface appears easier, should be sincere and incident specific, as well as positive, to ensure the intended impact. Table 12.3 above provides a summary of the information about effective and ineffective feedback based on the research reviewed.

Receiving feedback

Receiving feedback can be difficult, particularly if the information feels like a personal criticism or the interpretation of the facts and context seem misguided or inaccurate. The individual receiving the feedback should firstly listen without interruption; resisting the temptation to defend, clarify or dispute, to ensure all the facts and information is relayed and this information has been absorbed. Clarify any misunderstandings; add additional information which may be missing. Ask further questions and paraphrase to ensure you have interpreted and understood what has been said. Take the opportunity to discuss your perspective objectively and then describe the impact this information has had on you. Decide what learning opportunities there are and agree these. If it is appropriate, thank the individual for their insights.

Additional tips for receiving feedback

- Commit to listening and learning in all feedback situations.
- Monitor your non-verbal response.
- Relax, breathe and speak slowly in an even tone.
- Observe your emotional reaction in the moment.
- Create additional time to think by asking for time to reflect.
- Be comfortable with silence and pauses.
- Look for the important message(s).
- Be open to what you can learn.
- Be attentive – summarise in your own words.
- Accept positive feedback with thanks.
- Accept feedback for what it is – information.
- Remember that all feedback is subjective.
- Be aware of the 'filters' you may be listening with.
- Keep out of your own head and focused in the moment.
- Keep asking 'what else?'
- Evaluate the feedback before responding.
- Accept the impact of your behaviour as the reality for that individual; it doesn't mean that you have to agree with it.
- Let people know how the feedback has been helpful.
- Thank the individual for spending the time they took to prepare and present the feedback.

ACTIVITY **12.1**

Responses to feedback

Think about how you typically respond to feedback. How will this influence your coaching style?

Feedback assessment

Two sources of feedback that can be particularly useful when coaching are 360-degree feedback assessments and emotional intelligence tests.

360-degree feedback assessments

360-degree assessments can be used as a tool to measure performance and effectiveness in the workplace. This multi-rated, multi-source questionnaire provides feedback from the individuals a coachee interacts with – peers, subordinates, mentors, line managers and others. The coachee also completes a self-assessment and the results are collated into one report.

360-degree questionnaires can be bought off the shelf, with a focus on leadership behaviours, or developed to measure locally identified behaviours and competencies. The reports are usually computer generated and include a minimum of eight raters, one being the individual's line manager (see Holroyd and Brown, 2011)

McDowell (2010) suggests that they can be a useful foundation of information, especially when used in conjunction with coaching. However, she suggests that while useful, feedback from several sources can be just as biased and subjective and warns of the adverse impact relating promotions and pay rises to such tools.

Used well, they are an excellent mechanism to help provide detailed insights for the coachee of their impact at work. To avoid 360-degree reports being consigned to the drawer requires purposeful coaching feedback and the setting of realistic development targets which should be reviewed and progress evaluated. Indeed, feedback effectiveness improves if processes are supported by follow up coaching (Smither *et al.*, 2005).

Emotional intelligence tests in coaching

Like the 360-degree assessment, these tests can provide a wealth of information to support an individual's development. According to Caruso and Salovey (2008: 151) 'emotional intelligence is the ability to accurately and adaptively perceive, use, understand and manage emotions'. The capacity to identify emotions is crucial to fruitful interpersonal communications.

Awareness of an individual's emotional 'strengths and weaknesses' is extremely useful, and implementing strategies to compensate for a deficit in an 'emotional ability' is equally helpful in developing effective managers and leaders (Caruso and Salovey, 2008). Coaching provides the medium to further develop an individual's emotional intelligence.

Emotional intelligence tests can be a crucial resource, providing information that is not identified by other assessments. According to Caruso and Salovey, emotional intelligence review findings 'can stimulate deep, productive and difficult conversations in the coaching relationship as many people are poorly equipped to gauge their own emotional abilities' (2008: 169).

There are many psychometric tests which can be used in coaching, from Myers Briggs Type Inventory (MBTI) which is used to focus on 'character issues', 'problem solving', 'team development' and 'influencing' to Klob's learning styles approach (CIPD, 2010: 12). All offer additional information about the coachee.

Both of the above tests, however, can be used not only to identify learning goals but also to provide an ongoing assessment of progress made. Tracking progress is an integral component of coaching.

Tracking progress

O'Connor and Lages (2004) suggest that receiving feedback from the coachee is an important part of checking progress and that the established milestones and goals are on track or have been met. Coachees can be well intentioned and walk out the door overcommitted and too optimistic at what they can achieve. Detecting and helping individuals work through this tendency will certainly help them in present and future roles.

The measuring of progress, the specifics of how and when, should form part of the goal setting discussions, and may be as simple as, 'how will you measure progress?' Encouraging someone to set benchmarks and milestones can be helpful to chunk goals into more manageable achievements.

O'Connor and Lages (2004: 31) recommend the following questions:

- How will you know that you have achieved your goal?
- What milestones will you set up along the way?
- How will you know you are on track for this goal?
- How often will you check that you are on track?

If progress towards the goal requires a contribution from other individuals, it is important to factor this into the progress updates and to encourage the coachee to ensure that all aspects are on target and coach them to do this successfully.

This leads to the next important section on handling difficult conversations.

Section 13
Difficult conversations

This section explores conversations that are anticipated to be difficult. The structure of difficult conversations is explored and guidance offered as to how to convert these to learning conversations. Four main categories of difficult conversations are explored in detail.

Introducing difficult conversations

Difficult Conversations by Stone *et al.* (1999) reminds us that difficult conversations are often about what really 'matters the most' and are an inevitable part of communication. They would describe difficult conversations as opportunities to really learn about someone else.

Individuals experience and see the world differently; a theme discussed earlier. They choose what to remember, what to ignore, what to pay attention to and search for references to further reinforce their beliefs. The individual's daily rules to follow in life are formed in this way.

McDowall (2008) suggests that people do not always understand feedback and often are only interested in the positive information. Invariably, people like providing and receiving encouragement and praise.

According to the research, McDowall (2008: 41) advises that it is particularly important when criticising in any way that concrete examples are provided and care is taken to concentrate on the 'specific behaviours, and not the person'. She also acknowledges that no one really likes giving criticism and recommends that the coach reflects on their own style of providing this type of feedback in coaching supervision.

Three conversations

Stone *et al.* (1999: 7), suggest that 'each difficult conversation is really three conversations'.

1. 'The "What happened?" conversation'
   Difficult conversations involve a degree of 'disagreement about what has, or should happen', 'who did what', 'who's right' and 'who's to blame'?
2. 'The Feelings conversation'
   'Are my feelings valid, appropriate, should I acknowledge or deny them, put them on the table'? 'I'm under pressure'. They advise that these feelings leak out and are often 'not addressed directly'.
3. 'The Identity conversation'
   'This is the conversation we each have with ourselves about what the situation means to us'. The debate may include whether we are competent or incompetent, a good or bad person and whether it will impact on our self-image or wellbeing.

Stone *et al.* (1999) believe that to be effective with difficult conversations, the individual needs to be comfortable with each conversation simultaneously, operating across all three of them, and understanding fully the potential impact of each one.

They suggest that even if an individual becomes an expert there are certain challenges in each of the three conversations that cannot be changed. Identifying 'what happened', for example, will always have an element of missing information and there will be 'emotionally charged' events that will 'feel threatening', putting 'identity at risk'.

What can be changed, however, is how an individual responds. Fundamental issues which get in the way are the concepts of 'I am right, you are wrong' and who is to blame. Moving away from the 'truth assumption', or blame, shifts the purpose from 'proving we are right to understanding the perceptions, interpretations and values of both sides' (Stone *et al.*, 1999: 10). Focusing on blame also prevents explorations of why things went wrong and how these can be corrected.

According to Stone *et al.* (1999) the 'identity conversation' is always difficult because it is about what an individual is saying to themselves and, importantly:

Anytime a conversation feels difficult it is in part precisely because it is about you.

(1999: 15)

Resisting imparting information to an individual 'to get them to do or be what we want' is integral to 'moving towards a learning conversation' which involves understanding what has occurred from the 'other person's' point of view to share and appreciate the feelings involved and to work together as a way forward (Stone *et al.*, 1999: 16).

They suggest that 'it doesn't mean that all views are equally valid or that it's wrong to have strongly held beliefs' (p43).

The three conversations revisited

'The "What happened?" conversation'

The main rule here is to not 'assume' an individual's intention, abandon blame, and to disentangle impact from intent. They suggest asking three questions:

1. *Actions* – 'What did the other person actually say or do?'
2. *Impact* – 'What was the impact of this on me?'
3. *Assumption* – 'Based on this impact, what assumptions am I making about what the other person intended?'

'The Feelings conversation'

Feelings must be addressed and not 'bottled' up as they 'poison' relationships and are often the 'substance of the problem'. The following approach is advocated:

1. *Sort feelings* – Find your feelings. Accusations hide strong feelings.
2. *Negotiate with your feelings* – Amend your thinking, by reassessing the facts and assumptions and map your contribution to the problem.
3. *Share feelings not judgements* – Putting feelings into words, not evaluating yours or other people's emotions; instead, listen without judgement.

'The Identity conversation'

Stone *et al.* (1999) advise that 'difficult conversations confront others', but also us, in that our identity is challenged. They suggest avoiding the following:

1. *All or nothing* – I am competent, I am not competent.
2. *Denial* – Clinging to a purely positive identity leaves no place for negative feedback in our self-concept.
3. *Hyperbole* – Exaggeration and flipping; if I'm not completely competent, then I'm completely incompetent.
4. *Letting criticism define you* – Know your identity and accept yourself.

To gain 'balance' when an individual's 'identity' has been unsettled, Stone *et al.* suggest:

1. Don't try to control the other person's responses.
2. Prepare for their likely response.
3. Get perspective by thinking of yourself months or years in the future, long after the conflict has subsided.
4. Take needed breaks.
5. Remember the other individual is simultaneously having their own identity struggles with the conversation.

Learning conversations

To convert a difficult conversation into a learning conversation, Stone *et al.* (1999) suggest:

- Processing three issues, feelings, identity and distortions, or gaps in perception.
- Precluding difficult conversations if the 'real issue is inside you', the problem can be eliminated by changing your actions or your purpose in having the conversation is not clear or attainable.
- Allowing sufficient time for difficult conversations, 'don't hit and run'.
- 'Learning the other person's story', articulate your thoughts and feelings.
- Working on solving the problem together.
- Starting a difficult conversation in the third person, objective; invite the other individual as a partner to engage in problem solving.
- When delivering bad news, say it up front.
- Listening, paraphrasing using their words, repeat, acknowledge and keep eye contact.
- Being curious and genuine.
- Being aware of your internal dialogue/internal voice or self-talk.
- Using inquiry and open-ended questions.
- Speaking directly; clearly give them your story, targeted to them as a unique individual using visual and auditory cues, charts and metaphors to match their preferences.
- Taking the lead, reframe unhelpful expressions, accusations into intentions and impacts, blame as an equal contribution. Reframe 'what's wrong with you' statements as 'what's going on for them'.
- Choosing 'And . . .' stance.
- Validating the other's view and explain the importance of your own.

- If the conversation gets 'stuck', listen.
- Combining brainstorming of protracted issues.
- If no resolution is reached ask 'what standards ought to guide such an issue?'

Putting it all together

In order to conduct difficult conversations Stone *et al.* (1999) suggest:

1. Preparing for a difficult conversation.
2. Remembering the three conversations: 'what happened, feeling and identity'.
3. Deciding whether to have the conversation.
4. Starting with the objective third party stance, framing the problem.
5. Exploring both stories, reframe as needed to keep constructive.
6. Addressing any issues as they arise.
7. If no agreement, agree standards for what a solution should look like.
8. Keeping communication open.

Typical difficult conversations

There are a number of difficult conversations or encounters in coaching; some of these are discussed below and further explored as coaching conversations in Appendix 5. Typical 'difficult conversations' include the following:

- blocks in development – 'feeling stuck';
- an individual who is not performing;
- someone who is angry;
- someone is self-sabotaging or procrastinating.

Blocks in development

A 'block' can be described as the issue(s) preventing the coachee from progressing from the present state to achieving the identified outcomes or objectives. These can include barriers created by other individuals, but for the purpose of this discussion we will concentrate on the individual's internal mechanisms often presented to the coach as the coachee being 'stuck'.

Hawkins and Smith (2010: 235) depict in Table 13.1 how Heron's intervention styles can be used to help with a coachee who is 'stuck'.

They suggest that if an individual feels emotional or 'anxious' about undertaking something because of a previously bad experience, to explore using the cathartic intervention.

Flaherty (2010) reminds us that feeling stuck can present in many forms including: the same patterns of response, repeating over at work, or in an individual's personal life. He describes this as incredibly frustrating for the coachee, creating secondary symptoms of blaming others and self, becoming cynical which results in the amplification of a negative internal voice. He believes the fundamental cause of someone feeling this way is being 'unheld', and describes this as: 'lonely, misunderstood, out of place, unseen, unloved and abandoned'.

His remedy is to get the individual to see that they are 'only looking at life from one angle' and stress that 'in every moment the world is holding us' and to help the coachee to build 'exquisite self-care' for themselves (p152).

Table 13.1 Potential blockage and interventions using Heron's six interventions

Diagnosis	Intervention style	Facilitative
• Lack of confidence	• Supportive	
• Locked 'in the box'	• Catalytic	
• Feelings getting in the way	• Cathartic	
Diagnosis	**Intervention style**	**Authoritative**
• Needing a new awareness	• Confronting	
• Don't have necessary information	• Informative	
• Can't choose direction	• Prescriptive	

An individual is not performing

There may be many reasons for someone not performing. A 'solution focused' approach may help. This is a model which concentrates on an individual's 'competencies' instead of their 'deficits', their 'strengths rather than their weaknesses, their possibilities rather than their limitations' (Megginson and Clutterbuck, 2010: 91).

The coach identifies with the coachee occasions when they are performing well, establishing what's significant at those times. This builds a repertoire of understanding of when, and what, creates the optimum environment for the individual's best performance.

Flaherty (2010) would suggest the following exercise of self-observation:

Objective: to become more aware of what is and what is not being accomplished.

Stop twice in the day, at midday and at the end:

What specific, observable outcomes did I produce?

What excuses, stories or justifications do I have for not producing the outcomes I said I would produce?

What events, people or personal limitations got in the way of these outcomes?

How do I feel about what I have observed here?

Not performing may be about 'competing commitments'. Meggison and Clutterbuck (2010) provide the following example:

Commitment	*'I am committed to managing my time better and having a better work/life balance.'*
Behaviour	*'What I'm doing that prevents my commitment from being more fully realised is working weekends, over preparing and procrastinating.'*
Competing commitment	*'I may also be committed to doing perfect work.'*
Big assumption	*'I assume that if I'm not perfect, I'll be rejected.'*

The 'big assumption' in this case becomes the 'limiting belief'; working on this belief is crucial to improving the coachee's performance. This is particularly the case if an individual appears to be working hard or distracted in activity but their outputs don't match.

The language used can provide important clues to deeply held beliefs or assumptions. According to Hill (cited in Megginson and Clutterbuck, 2010) these are characterised by the following words:

never	could	couldn't
always	should	shouldn't
everyone	ought	oughtn't

She suggests that focusing on the assumptions until the 'core' belief is revealed is the approach to take.

Someone who is angry

If an individual is becoming angry about something, Starr (2011: 92) would suggest shifting their attention to the 'present moment' and ask the following questions:

- 'So, what seems important about that right now?'
- 'Can you think of any other information that would be relevant about that for us here, now?'
- 'What else do you want to say about that to me right now?'

The amount of stress in someone's life can impact upon how frequently an individual is angry. An individual who is chronically or acutely stressed will react to small events with hostility. Invariably stress can cause anger and anger cause further stress. If something is perceived not right, this can trigger an angry outburst. Therefore it is important to establish if the anger fits the situation. If it does not, care and attention needs to be directed at reducing the stress by helping the individual look after their well-being. (See Appendix 5 for an example of how to coach someone who needs to establish a better work/life balance.)

Bossons *et al.* (2009) advises that anger should be treated as a legitimate reaction and the individual helped to express what is underneath it.

Flaherty (2010) would suggest the following exercise of self-observation:

Objective: to become more aware of an individual's feelings at work, any strong emotional responses.

Stop twice in the day, at midday and at the end:

What was my strongest feeling at work today?

What triggered this feeling?

What conversation or activity was I engaged in?

How did I respond/react to this feeling?

What actions will I take from what I observed?

Someone is self-sabotaging or procrastinating

In terms of self-sabotage, Stephenson (2010) has identified that people do this for all sorts of reasons and listed above (on pages 91 and 92) are all the 'BUTs' that accompany this problem.

Borg (2010) would agree and describes self-sabotage as connected to negative self-talk, for example, 'I'll never be able to do that . . . I can't spare the time for that', and that 'self-sabotaging beliefs serve to reinforce our reasons for inaction' (p72).

Hardingham *et al.* (2009: 112) describe procrastinating as 'thinking in order to avoid action'. Molden (2007) links procrastination with 'fear' and suggests asking the coachee 'what's important about this task?' (p220). He advocates using the 'orange circle' technique which is detailed in Appendix 6.

Megginson and Clutterbuck (2010: 150) remind us that procrastination can become a 'habit'; and suggest breaking this by asking the question: 'When would be the best time to procrastinate about this?'

Borg (2010: 117) would link stress as a contributing factor to procrastination and details four approaches to dealing with stress as the 4 'A's:

1. Adapt
2. Accept
3. Avoid
4. Alter

Each requires change either in an individual's reaction or situation, for example, *adapt* and *accept* (which require a change in the individual's reaction) or *alter* and *avoid* (which necessitates a 'change in the situation').

Flaherty (2010) would suggest the following exercise of self-observation:

Objective: to become more aware of an individual's feelings, thoughts and reactions concerning completion and take action from what is learnt.

Stop twice in the day, at midday and at the end:

What did I complete? Why was it important to complete this?

What did I leave incomplete? Why did I leave it so?

What do I currently feel compelled to complete? Why?

What will happen to me if I don't complete these things?

What did I learn from this exercise? What action will I take from what I learned?

There are not only issues for the coachee but also traps or pitfalls for the coach in coaching conversations.

Section 14
Remaining resourceful and developing practice

Coaching, while potentially enriching for everyone involved, can be challenging, tiring and occasionally draining, especially for the coach. Without care it is easy for the coach to fall into well-known traps; to fail to exercise self-care and for their practice to decline. This section identifies common coaching traps and looks at options for professional development.

Common 'coaching traps'

There are six common coaching traps.

The coach needing to be brilliant

The idea that the coach needs to have all the answers and look good can be a real risk according to Kline (2007). She goes on to suggest that this gets in the way, and cuts short the exchange, before real deep thinking can take place. It can also be intimidating for the coachee and stifling for their development. The focus of the coaching encounter should be on the coachee and not the coach. Needing to be right is very similar to needing to be 'brilliant' and both require a letting go of this requirement (Starr, 2011).

Remedy: to consciously set aside any feelings as a coach and to focus on the coachee or individual. The coach can explore this tendency with a supervisor.

The coach wanting to help/to rescue

While wanting to help has a natural link with coaching, it becomes a problem when this need results in a wish to 'control' (Hardingham *et al.*, 2009). The coach may be resolute that they know the answer(s), resulting in the coach forcing their approach or view on the individual.

A strong desire to help burdens the coachee and can create 'dependency' (Hardingham *et al.*, 2009). It can also cloud the coach's ability to create the right kind of conversation for the individual to reach their own right answer. Individuals are ultimately responsible for themselves and, therefore, personal ownership is of paramount importance in achieving successful outcomes.

Remedy: to be aware of this trap and ensure that, as a coach, you are receiving supervision. Knowing yourself well and becoming clear of when this happens and remembering that it is not actually helping the individual.

The coach gets too involved

By trying to see, feel and understand where the coachee is coming from, the coach can become 'too involved' or 'too empathetic' and this can lead to a loss of effectiveness as a coach is not able to stay fully 'objective' (Bossons *et al.*, 2009: 62). It can also result in 'thinking for' rather than 'with' the individual.

Remedy: Bossons *et al.* (2009: 62) suggest that a coach should develop an 'optimal level of empathy' by being aware in the moment and should remember that it is unhelpful for the coach to become 'unresourceful' by getting too involved.

The coach wanting to pass on their wisdom

The coach falls into the trap of thinking they have experienced, or seen, a particular problem before and, therefore, they believe they know the answer. A premature solution-focused response can ensue, together with the coach unconsciously finding supporting evidence to match the conclusion reached. This prevents all the information being elicited and being fully discussed. No two incidents or experiences can ever be the same.

Remedy: the coach needs to be mindful of this pitfall and should compensate by being extra vigilant. Coaching supervision may also help to avoid this trap and provide a different perspective.

The coach wanting to play intellectual games

Solving so-called people puzzles can be an attractive intellectual game. Trying to be clever can overcomplicate, distract and move the coachee away from what really matters to them.

Remedy: to be self-aware in the moment and recognise if this is being played out; to remember that, often, less content in a question will produce a fuller answer from the coachee; and to be mindful that, as a coach, you are there for the individual.

The coach has their own 'limiting beliefs'

This may manifest as a result of something that has adversely happened to the coach. It can also be related to the coach feeling inadequate in comparison to the coachee, for example, less well paid or educated. Bossons *et al.* (2009: 61) remind us that this gets in the way of 'giving your best'.

Remedy: to recognise if this is happening and ask the question 'is this true?' (Bossons *et al.* 2009: 61). Continuing professional development and supervision can also help.

Managing state

An important component of being a coach is making sure that you are as resourceful as possible, which includes not coaching when too tired, stressed or upset. It is also important to be aware of what part of the day you are most productive and how to manage your state.

McDermott and Jago (2003) discuss the importance of understanding and recognising what emotional state the coach is in, for example, apprehensive, angry, frustrated, or simply feeling negative and preoccupied. Described as unresourceful states, although they can be fleeting changes in the coach's internal physiology, they 'produce external markers' (O'Connor, 2001: 72). These 'tell-tale' signs can leak out into the exchange and impact on the conversation.

For the coach this gets in the way of listening and thinking rationally and clearly. The coachee may have triggered the above negative feelings. McDermott and Jago (2003) suggest that you can learn to take control of your 'state' by changing what you are thinking about, becoming aware, acknowledging these feelings with the coachee, if appropriate, or simply to oneself, and getting curious will change the thoughts which are triggering the emotional response.

Being aware of states and recognising them in others also provides very useful information. For the coach reflecting later on what triggered the response is part of the continuous self-awareness and development process. Learning about an impact in the moment and seeing 'self' from different perspectives is developing 'self-reflexiveness', which McDermott and Jago (2010: 48) describe as being 'at the very heart of coaching'.

ACTIVITY **14.1**

Reflecting on coaching conversations

Reflect on each coaching session and notice what was uncomfortable. What went well? How will this influence your coaching style?

Continuing professional development and coaching

As with any training and development, it is important to continue the process of learning, practising and attaining additional skills. Hawkins and Smith refer to Tomlinson's (1993) definition of continuing professional development as:

> *The systematic maintenance, improvement and broadening of knowledge and skills and the development of personal qualities necessary for the execution of professional, managerial and technical duties throughout one's working life.*

> (2010: 134)

Hawkins and Smith (2010) stress the importance of supervision in continuing professional development.

Lee (2007: 151) refers to supervision as an: 'ongoing method for maintaining the quality of coaching', the effectiveness of which is 'dependent on the capacity of coaches to attend to the process of interactions as well as the content of their discussions'. Bossons *et al.* (2009) stress the significance of finding the right supervision for the coach, and Megginson and Clutterbuck (2009) discuss the distinct role the coachee can play in providing vital feedback to the coach.

Megginson and Clutterbuck (2009: 216) suggest the following questions to reflect upon before a supervision session:

- What is the psychological contract between you and your coachee, and you and your supervisor?
- How do you feel generally about your coaching?
- When did you feel moments of disconnect in the coaching conversation?
- What questions worked well? Less well?
- What questions did you not ask and why?

- Where do you feel least confident?
- What patterns do you notice in your reactions to the coachee?
- What challenge can you offer the supervisor?

The coach's ability to implement the 'self-observation' perspective is crucial in creating the space to reflect, to further build their self-awareness and gain additional insights. Supervision is an integral part of the process (Lee, 2007).

A 'coaching culture' has been defined by Hardingham *et al.* (2009: 184) as 'a culture where people coach each other all the time as a natural part of meetings, reviews and one to one discussions of all kinds'. It is not the exclusive domain of executives but part of everyday life; a leadership style that cultivates creativity and effective performance.

Hardingham *et al.* advocate that coaching is a 'common human activity' of 'assisted problem solving' and a 'normal part of what successful people and organisations do'. It is not a 'cosy culture' but one that requires skills to have 'difficult conversations' (2009: 190).

Tools and techniques

Megginson and Clutterbuck (2010: 3) described a technique as 'similar to models but in addition have a process for using the model attached to them', and provides the example of 'thinking, feeling, willing' as a model; the technique referred to 'head, heart and guts'. They describe tools as, 'devices which help us to talk about issues' (2010: 4). They warn that 'learning conversations' should drive the interaction and not the 'tool or technique'.

It is important when using any coaching tool to identify what need or needs the tool will fulfil, to have an appreciation and practised working knowledge of the tool so that it meets the desired requirements. The coach should avoid having a favourite tool; risking becoming too attached to an approach and making all encounters fit will narrow, rather than expand the exchange.

1. Six Thinking Hats – Edward de Bono

When to use: This is a good technique for looking at the implications of a decision from a number of different angles.

The six thinking hats encourage individuals to think in a more systematic and thorough way in addressing problems and issues (see Appendix 7). There are different types of thinking and a corresponding hat to match; this tool encourages individuals to think more effectively and deeply by deliberately concentrating on one type of thinking at a time.

An individual is encouraged to wear one colour of hat at a time; each hat represents a particular focus, for example, the red hat signifies feelings or gut reactions. It is a methodology to ensure all aspects are covered and provides a degree of objectivity.

Using a variety of approaches within thinking and problem solving allows the issue to be addressed from a variety of angles, thus servicing the needs of all individuals concerned. It can therefore reduce conflicts in groups or teams as the coloured hats are abstract figurative metaphors.

2. The neurological levels

When to use:

- To create rapport.
- To consider in a change context.
- To identify the level at which change needs to take place in order to be effective and lasting.
- Getting someone to think about a mission or purpose and their role can create profound insights and clarity for the individual.

The neurological levels model was created by Robert Dilts and is discussed in his book *Sleight of Mouth* (1999: 246).

Hardingham *et al.* (2009: 99) advocate using these levels 'to build rapport'. Molden (2007: 7) has adapted the levels to create what he describes as 'five levels of learning, communication and change'. These, he believes, are crucial in developing 'flexibility of thinking' and include the following:

1. identity or role;
2. values and beliefs;
3. capabilities;
4. behaviour;
5. environment;

The neurological levels are depicted in Appendix 8.

Identifying at what level a problem exists, whether it is at a capabilities or skill level or higher in the pyramid, for example, at the beliefs or values level, is important. Collapsing a 'limiting assumption or belief' at this level will change all the levels below. Implicitly changing an identity issue will correspondingly impact positively on all the levels below. An individual, for example, may be avoiding doing a task because of a capabilities issue: they have never written a report before. Identifying this and sending them on a report-writing course would alleviate this issue and the associated belief attached that they are no good at report writing.

Values would describe what you expect of self and how you describe yourself as a person, while your behaviour is what you do. Values and beliefs drive us and influence our capabilities and behaviour.

The neurological levels can also be used to ask a series of questions, for example, what does this level mean for you? Further exploration can increase the individual's insights about what is important to them and what they may be overlooking.

In a programme of change, each level can be scrutinised, for example:

- What is my purpose within this change?
- Who am I in relation to the planned change?
- What do these changes mean to my values and beliefs?
- What new skills and capabilities do I need? And how do I make the required changes?
- What behaviours do I need to change or consider?
- Where in the environment are these changes taking place?

3. Use of metaphors and stories

When to use:

- To help someone to better understand a situation.
- To reframe a difficult situation.
- To create sufficient detachment and safety for the coachee to explore and gain useful insights to effect change.

Megginson and Clutterbuck describe a metaphor as:

> *A powerful method of provoking both intellectual and emotional exploration of the dimensions of a situation. It enables learners to use their creative imagination to connect with aspects of the situation that they might otherwise neglect.*

> (2010: 55)

Matching the coachee's experience, especially at an 'emotional level, with strong imagery and language that captures the imagination' with the ability to 'explore choices' within the story, creates the foundations of an 'effective metaphor' (Megginson and Clutterbuck, 2010: 54).

Megginson and Clutterbuck advocate a three-step model for using metaphor to effect change.

> *Step 1*: Select a metaphor or story and place the coachee within the story. Determine their role and match as much of the context to the situation, which includes roles for the individuals involved.

> *Step 2*: The coach asks, for example, when and how parts of this story have been 'played out in real life'. If some aspects do not fit the metaphor, they are recorded and set aside for a follow-up discussion. The exchange then examines how the metaphor has developed over time and is expected to 'evolve in the future'. Exploring the metaphor from the differing aspect of each of the characters can provide rich connections and insights.

> *Step 3*: Ask the coachee to elicit the learning from the metaphor and what details had the most significant impact. Establish what parts of the metaphor they would like to change.

> (2010: 55)

4. The meaning of 'Yes' and Danger? What's dangerous about that?

When to use:

- To establish or calibrate the level of commitment.
- To establish what is holding someone's commitment back.

The meaning of 'Yes' (Hill, cited in Megginson and Clutterbuck, 2010: 141)
It asks the individual to be as truthful as possible in identifying from the list below where their level of commitment lies.

10. I am totally determined to achieve this, whatever the cost.
9. I am very determined to do this and I'm prepared to make major sacrifices to do so.
8. I will make this my number one priority.
7. This will be one of my key priorities.

6. It's very important to me.
5. It's quite important to me.
4. I feel obligated to do this.
3. I'm not sure this is what I really want.
2. I'm quite reluctant.
1. Over my dead body!

Danger? What's dangerous about that?

Hill (cited in Megginson and Clutterbuck, 2010) reminds us that it is easy for individuals to 'catastrophise' and see the worst in things, especially when they are under pressure and stressed. This exercise is simple, the coachee is asked 'why was that dangerous?' and then takes the answer and repeats the question. The question, 'why was that dangerous?' is repeated over to identify any underlying issues or to reveal what was perceived to be dangerous is in fact not the case. The example provided by Hill (p143):

- It is dangerous because I feel pressured.
- She is trying to psychoanalyse me.
- She takes things too far.
- She becomes critical of me.
- I end up worrying.
- It isn't dangerous at all – in fact it's useful.

5. Nancy Kline's Thinking Exercise

When to use:

- To stimulate new thinking, insights and creativity.
- For change management; to explore what may have been overlooked.
- To examine patterns and connections not previously identified.
- To really get to the bottom of an issue.

Kline suggests that 'the most tenacious block to new ideas is a limiting assumption'. She suggests that there are three types of 'assumption':

1. a fact ('I am not the boss; he is');
2. a possible fact ('The boss might laugh at me or think I am stupid');
3. a bedrock assumption about the self ('I am stupid') or ('It is not all right to get it wrong').

(2007: 167)

Other limiting bedrock assumptions of how life works may include the following:

- 'I have to have all the answers.'
- 'It isn't possible.'
- 'Change is difficult and takes a long time.'
- 'What doesn't kill you makes you stronger.'
- 'People like me are not important.'
- 'Talking about a problem means you are weak.'
- 'Ordinary people cannot affect large social systems.'
- 'You can't have it both ways.'

(2007: 171)

Kline, however, believes that limiting assumptions can be removed through listening and asking incisive questions. A question compels an individual to answer and, therefore, to think. Once a limiting assumption is removed the individual is free to think creatively (see Appendix 9).

6. The wheel of life

When to use:

- To identify an area of life an individual wants to set and achieve goals.
- To work with work/life balance building a sense of perspective.
- To help to identify areas of an individual's life which are important.
- To help to re-establish priorities.
- Increase self-awareness of what is important to the individual.

The wheel of life is a common coaching tool; it demonstrates what is important to an individual, which is not always obvious in a busy and frenetic life. The roles an individual plays in their life and what they feel would be ideal.

1. Use the circle in Appendix 10 – the labels can be changed and segments added to include areas which are deemed as additionally significant, for example, confidence, organisation, creativity, team, colleague, community, sports and fitness.
2. Assess each segment and reflect on how much attention you are currently devoting to that area in your life, reflect on why and what are the consequences. Consider which areas you are most accomplished in, or are the most significant and important and consider why this is. Which areas are priorities for you at the moment? Which areas are aligned to your goals and which are not?
3. Along the spokes for each area place a dot to represent how satisfied you are. Use the scale 1 to 5 to help (1 being the lowest score and 5, the outer ring, being the most satisfied).
4. Next join up the dots and observe; how round is your wheel, does it look balanced? Which areas are you most satisfied with and which require attention? The ideal is to have a large round wheel which is balanced to avoid a bumpy life.
5. Now consider your ideal; what degree of attention would you need to devote to each area? Plot a new dot along the spoke to identify the ideal and then join the dots up. There are two visible patterns, one representing the current situation and the other the ideal.
5. Identify the gaps, what do you most want to change, what area(s) do you want to work on, in terms of achieving your goals, which should you concentrate on? What top three things would make the biggest difference in your life? Are there any tensions, and how would you overcome these?
6. Develop a plan of action; you may need to identify things you should stop doing in order to concentrate on the other areas. What daily actions do you need to take? Make a commitment by writing down and signing the plan.

ACTIVITY **14.2**

Reflecting on tools used

Keep a log of the tools used. Monitor when you have used a tool and how effective it was.

Appendix 1
Further definitions of coaching

Coaching is a conversation, or a series of conversations, that one person has with another. The person who is the coach intends to produce a conversation that will benefit the other person.

(Starr, 2011: 4)

We look at coaching as an approach, it is for anyone who seeks to gain, or help develop, greater personal mastery.

(McDermott and Jago, 2010: 2)

A structured two-way process in which individuals develop skills and achieve defined competencies through assessment, guided practical experience and regular feedback.

(Parsloe, 1995: 1)

Coaching is partnering with clients in a thought-provoking and creative process that inspires them to maximise their personal and professional potential.

(International Coach Federation, 2008)

Collaborative, solution-focused and systematic process which is aimed at enhancing performance, self-directed learning and well-being.

(Grant, 2003: 275)

Psychological skills and methods are employed in a one-on-one relationship to help someone become a more effective manager or leader. These skills are typically applied to specific present-moment work-related issues in a way that enables this client to incorporate them into his or her permanent management or leadership repertoire.

(Peltier, 2010: xxxi)

A coach is someone who helps another person or group of people articulate and achieve their goals, through conversation with them.

(Hardingham et al., 2009: ix)

Coaching relates primarily to performance improvement (often over a short term) in a specific skill area.

(Megginson and Clutterbuck, 2010: 4)

Appendix 2
Johari Window exercise

There are 56 adjectives listed below. The individual, their peers and other people who may know them are asked to select six adjectives which describe the individual. The adjectives are then mapped onto the grid in the following panes:

Pane 1

The same adjectives which have been chosen by both the individual and their peers are matched. These words are then placed in pane 1. This is often called the 'open area' (what is known by self and known to others).

Pane 2

The adjectives which have been selected by the peers and are not in the individual's pile are placed in this pane; this is the individual's 'blind spot'.

Pane 3

The adjectives chosen by the individual but not the peers, the hidden words 'known to self', can be disclosed by the subject if they wish and are placed in pane three.

Pane 4

Will now contain all the adjectives not selected by anyone, representing the 'unknown'.
Adjectives to select from:

able	dependable	intelligent	patient	sensible
accepting	dignified	introverted	powerful	sentimental
adaptable	energetic	kind	proud	shy
bold	extroverted	knowledgeable	quiet	silly
brave	friendly	logical	reflective	smart
calm	giving	loving	relaxed	spontaneous
caring	happy	mature	religious	sympathetic
cheerful	helpful	modest	responsive	tense
clever	idealistic	nervous	searching	trustworthy
complex	independent	observant	self-assertive	warm
confident	ingenious	organised	self-conscious	witty
wise				

Appendix 3
GROW model – some example questions to ask

GROW   **'GOAL'**

What is it that you want to change?

How do you want things to change?

How might you benefit?

What do you want the outcome to be?

What is the goal of this meeting/discussion?

How much time do we have?

What are you specifically looking for from me?

What do you want to accomplish in the short term, medium and long term?

What one or two things would make a real difference to how you feel if you concentrated on them and disregarded everything else?

What are your goal(s)?

So your goal at work would be?

What are you most proud of?

How has this problem affected you?

Deep inside what do you absolutely want from your work life?

Describe to me in some detail what a typical perfect working day would be like?

How can you see yourself benefiting?

What would be the consequences of doing the exact opposite of what you would normally do here?

What is the most important thing for you?

What would your 'best self' say to you and advise you to do?

What do you most hope for?

What does success look like and feel like for you?

When do you want to achieve the goal by?

Is that positive, challenging, and attainable?

Could you say more?

How will you measure it?

What would be a milestone along the way?

How much control do you have over this goal?

When you've got there, what will you see, hear, feel and do differently?

Imagine it is next Monday/next week/year (choose a timescale that seems appropriate). You have achieved your goal and you are now able to describe the outcome. How are you feeling?

GROW **'REALITY'** (WHAT, WHEN, WHERE, HOW MUCH, HOW OFTEN)

What would be your specific role in achieving this goal?

What is stopping you now?

Can you see any dangers here?

Who knows who should know?

Can you describe more fully your concerns?

What is real for you now? Or what is your reality?

Who is involved?

What have you done about this so far?

What outcomes did you produce?

What is happening internally and externally?

What are the major barriers to finding a way forward?

How much do you feel is within your control?

What is the disappointment? What is related to this?

What are the consequences of not achieving your goals?

What sort of thing could address that concern?

What else bothers you? And what else? And – tell me some more?

What sort of people and activities do you enjoy most at work?

What is it about those people and those activities that you like?

If you had to state a purpose for your life what would it be?

How do you react, normally?

What do you actually really want to say . . .?

Have you ever had a problem like this previously? How did you deal with it then?
Was it successful?

What resources do you need?

Do you have all the information you require?

Who could you ask for help?

Who else is involved with this issue?

More specifically what have you tried?

What were you attempting to accomplish?

GROW **'OPTIONS'**

What is useful about this, can you expand further?

What do you think someone else would do?

What would your 'best self' do?

What are the advantages and disadvantages you see in this proposal?

What options do you have here?

What else could you do?

What if . . .?

If you knew what the answer would be, what would it be?

What are the benefits and costs of each?

What would you do differently now?

How do you feel about it?

What would be the benefits . . . and what would you lose?

Anything else . . . and . . . ?

How will such and such a body react?

How could that affect you?

Can you identify any risks?

What is a possible alternative?

Suppose you approached it in this particular way? What could happen?

How do you feel about that?

What do you think the consequences would be if you did . . .?

Who else could support you?

Who else might have something to add?

Have your covered all the possible options?

Who do you know that may have had a similar experience to this?

How could you do things differently?

What can you learn from this?

From where you are at this moment what could be a first step?

I am thinking about doing this, would this be helpful?

Would you like another suggestion?

GROW   **'WILL'**

What will you commit to do and by when?

What are you going to do?

Will this meet your goal?

When are you going to do it?

What obstacles could you face?

How will you measure success?

What will be your first action?

Who needs to know?

What support will you seek out?

How will you go about getting that support?

What other considerations might you have?

On a scale of 1–10, what is the probability of your succeeding or completing this task?

What stops it being a 10?

What could stop you progressing?

What do you think is realistic?

What else will you do?

Tell me specifically what actions you will take?

What should you do right now?

What will you do to make sure you stay on track?

Is there anything else you want to say?

Appendix 4
Enhancing motivation

Source of motivation	Do	Don't
Independence	• Provide privacy and favour individual rather than group interaction. • Listen, don't tell and ask for advice – participative management is important. • Emphasise similarity and congruence between personal and organisational goals. • Provide opportunities for leadership in the organisation.	• Recommend or breed conformity. • Fail to give positive reinforcement.
Recognition	• Ensure that recognition is sincere and develops over time (a desire for recognition is almost universal). • Balance constructive criticism with praise. • Provide opportunities to participate in decisions, when appropriate.	• Devalue recognition by being insincere. • Ignore an individual who is motivated by recognition.
Achievement	• Be available for advice but help only when asked. • Encourage individuals to set their own goals. • Compare results with goals and highlight specific rather than general issues. • Provide new challenges.	• Supervise too closely or impose your own standards. • Set goals. • Expect conformity.
Leisure time	• Consider how leisure time can be enhanced by improving performance.	• Ignore work schedules and deadlines. • Intrude on leisure time.
Power	• Give individual attention, listening rather than telling. • Recognise when individuals ask for feedback but don't really want it.	

Source of motivation	Do	Don't
	• Help individuals understand that they're needed.	• Fail to give recognition or criticise too heavily. • Fail to highlight how individuals are succeeding.
Prestige	• Encourage individuals to get involved in a range of activities. • Support the individuals, introducing them to people, resources and situations that will advance their prospects. • Provide genuine and sincere praise – recognise that if praise is given to a group, it may limit an individual's growth.	• Ignore the significance of the trappings of success.
Money	• Link objectives with commission and remuneration. • Consider introducing a performance-related bonus system.	• Don't ignore the significance of money and other forms of remuneration.
Pressure	• Agree intermediate and final deadlines. • Provide focus and set challenging goals. • Encourage a work/life balance. • Be patient and provide continued support and reassurance.	• Overreact. • Ignore causes of concern.
Self-esteem	• Encourage people with low esteem by recognising achievements. • Avoid threats and set realistic goals. • Set challenging goals and delegate both responsibility and authority.	• Ignore the need for guidance, independence, recognition and support.
Family life	• Show genuine interest and acceptance of family life. • Recognise the value of social interaction.	• Become over-involved in family issues or play at being a counsellor.
Security	• Ensure consistency. • Provide supervision in a predictable comfortable way. • Set goals.	• 'Rock the boat' without careful consideration of the likely consequences.
Personal growth	• Channel activities and effort. • Focus on an individual's feelings. • Provide specific rather than general suggestions for progress.	• Ignore the need for recognition, practical support and positive reinforcement.

Source: Bossons *et al.* (2009: 150)

Appendix 5
Real-life examples

1. Coaching someone who is not performing

Consideration needs to be given as to whether the individual has the capability to deliver the work that is required of them. If they are not, then coaching would be inappropriate. Coaching should not be part of a formal performance management process; this should instead be undertaken with the assistance of the human resources department. Once you have established that a coaching conversation may be helpful, below are some questions which could be used once rapport is established.

Establishing the goal

- Let's talk about the work you completed this week. What was the key thing(s) you wanted to achieve?
- How do you think you did?
- What feedback have you had from the team, the team leader or anybody else about this work?
- We need to talk some more about the specifics. How, for example, could this week's referral sheet be improved?

Establishing the reality

- If there were key things that you wanted to achieve this week, to what extent do you think you achieved them?
- Would it be useful for us to go through some of these specific things?
- It sounds like, while there are a few areas that are being completed appropriately, there are others that are not?
- It seems that you may be running out of time to complete the referral sheets, is this correct?
- What will happen if time continues to be an issue?
- What effect will this have on the rest of the team?

Establishing the options

- What ideas do you have for addressing this issue?
- What else could you do?
- What would you do differently now?
- How do you feel about that?
- What would be the benefits . . . and what would you lose?

- Anything else you want to say?
- Would you like another suggestion, something you could do to achieve the reports in time? Would that help?
- Is there anything that might hinder you achieving your goal?
- What is preventing you right now from achieving this?

Establish what they will do

- What do you plan to do next to get back on track? What's the first step you want to take?
- What obstacles might you face?
- When do you want to achieve this by?
- What support would you like from me?
- When shall we meet again to check on how things are going?

2. Coaching someone who is demotivated

Helping individuals feel motivated at work can be complex. Bossons *et al.* (2009) describe eight important principles of motivation: (1) be motivated yourself; (2) select people who are highly motivated; (3) treat each individual as an individual; (4) set realistic and challenging targets; (5) remember that progress motivates; (6) create an environment that is motivating; (7) provide fair rewards; and (8) provide recognition.

Establishing the goal

- What are the main things that you like doing at work?
- What do you enjoy most about working here?
- How motivated on a scale of 1–10 do you feel at work (10 being completely)?
- Have you ever had a job you were totally engrossed by? What was it specifically about the job that made you feel that way?
- What are you absolutely passionate about?
- When do you feel most energised at work?
- Deep down, what do you really want from your work? What else . . . and what else . . . and if there was one thing more what would it be?

Establishing the reality

- What is stopping you being totally motivated at this moment?
- What is not happening?
- How much of this situation do you feel in control of?
- Is there anything else . . .?
- What would need to change in your work for you to be totally motivated?
- So what needs to happen?
- What one thing would make a difference?

Establishing the options

- If you could make any changes to your role to make it better what would they be?
- What options do you have?
- What could you do differently now?

- What else could you do?
- How do you feel about that?
- What would be the benefits?
- Can you see any risks?

Establish what they will do

- What is the first step you are going to take to make things better?
- When do you want to achieve this by?
- On a scale of 1–10 what is the likelihood of you achieving this?
- What would need to happen to make this a 10?
- What will you agree to do differently this week/next week/over the next month to address the issues you have identified?
- Who could help you achieve this goal?
- What support do you need from me?

3. Coaching someone who is struggling to maintain a work/life balance

While work/life issues may be a sign of wider and sometimes personal issues, there is an opportunity to explore what is happening and if there is anything that can be done to help the individual leave work on time.

Establishing the goal

- On a scale of 1–10 how happy are you with your work/life balance right now, with 10 being totally happy?
- I have noticed you are late leaving the office each night and are first in in the morning. Could you tell me more about what's going on for you?
- If I had a magic wand and could give you a perfect work/life balance what would that look like?
- What would this really mean to you?
- How do you want things to change?
- When you get there what will you see, feel, hear and do differently?

Establishing the reality

- What is stopping you having a perfect work/life balance?
- How would you prefer to be spending your time, in and out of the office?
- Is there something specific at work that is preventing you from managing to complete your work in office hours?
- What will be different, when you have your perfect work/life balance?
- How do your thoughts about a perfect work/life balance compare with what's really going on?

Establishing the options

- Has there ever been a time when you had a perfect work/life balance?
- What ideas do you have about what you might change to improve things?

- What have you already done?
- What different ways could you make the difference, change?
- How do you feel about that?
- What would be the benefits and is there anything you would lose?
- If you knew what the answer would be, what would it be?
- Anything else you want to say? Anything else . . .?
- How will your colleagues react?
- How will that affect you?
- Can you see any risks?

Establish what they will do

- What is the first step you are going to take to a better work/life balance?
- When do you want to achieve this by?
- On a scale of 1–10 what is your chance of achieving this?
- What will you agree to do differently this week/next week/over the next month to address the issues you have identified?
- Who could help you with this goal?

Appendix 6

Molden's Orange Circle Thinking

Use: To quickly reframe how someone is thinking.

Molden (2007) uses two shapes for this exercise, a blue square and an orange circle (p80 and p223). He suggests that the blue colour represents 'rules and regulations' and the corners of the square act as 'restrictions'. The orange colour of the circle, in contrast, represents 'energy and vitality' and the circle as a shape is about 'flow'.

- He advises the individual to think about something that they are procrastinating about and to capture what they are thinking and feeling on a blue square card.
- The individual should then take an orange pen and place a dot in the centre of the square while thinking of all the good things that will be realised as a result of completing the task. To also establish all the ways the task could be made more enjoyable, and for every positive thought, the individual should draw an orange circle around the dot, repeatedly drawing a circle for every positive thought until the card is full.
- He then suggests taking an orange circle and drawing a symbol on it to denote the new way of thinking about the task.
- If the individual feels ready, they can destroy the blue card.
- If not, the individual should be encouraged to recollect a time when they did successfully achieve a positive outcome for a task, and to notice the images associated with this, the intensity of the colour and the brightness. Get the individual to bring the image closer to them until the feelings get stronger and stronger; at the peak ask them to look at the blue square. They will feel differently about it and ready to move on.

Appendix 7
Edward de Bono's Six Thinking Hats

Six distinct states are identified and assigned a coloured hat:

White hat – information What information is available? What are the facts? What, when, where, how, who? Trends? Identify any information or data that is missing. Usually start with the white hat after the blue hat sets the scene.

Red hat – emotions Instinctive gut reactions or emotional feeling, intuition, hunches, don't justify. Use it to try to think about how others may react.

Black hat – negative/pessimistic Identify the drawbacks, barriers, disadvantages, 'devil's advocate', dangers, distractions, mismatches.

Yellow hat – positive/optimism Identify the positive points, advantages, benefits, way forward, reasons in favour.

Green hat – creativity Coming up with new ideas, possibilities, solutions, and thoughts without any criticism. Linking concepts and brainstorming ideas.

Blue hat – thinking Thinking about the process – the chairman or facilitator will wear this hat or it can be worn at the beginning or end of a meeting. It emphasises process control, identifies goals, actions, decisions made, summarising and the big picture. To slow the process down and think in an orderly way.

(Source: Edward de Bono, *Six Thinking Hats*, 2002)

Benefits:

- Shorter and more productive meetings.
- Reduce conflict.
- Look at decisions and problems systematically.
- Achieve results.
- Generate more and better ideas.
- Think clearly.
- Improve team results.
- Solve problems, innovate and create.

Appendix 8

Using neurological levels – created by Robert Dilts

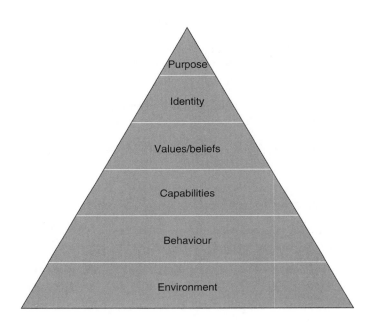

Appendix 9

Time to think – listen to ignite the human mind. Adapted from Nancy Kline (2007)

Thinking exercise

1. 'What do you want to think about?' Listen carefully, paying full attention.
2. 'Is there anything more you think or feel, or want to say or tell me about this?'
3. 'What do you want the session to achieve at this point?' (Repeat the goal using the individual's own exact words).
4. 'What are you assuming (that is stopping you achieving that goal)?'
5. 'What else? . . . and what else . . . if there was anything else, what would it be?'
6. Which do you think is the most limiting assumption?
7. When you believe you have identified the main limiting belief, remove it by suggesting the opposite is true . . . 'How would things be different if . . .' (replace the limiting assumption with the opposite).
8. If you knew that (new, freeing assumption) . . . what ideas would you have towards your goal?
9. Ask an incisive question, for example: 'If things could be exactly right for you in this situation, how would they have to change?'
10. Create an incisive question from question 8, if you knew that (add the freeing assumption) to the original goal and listen for the incisive question. Capture and write this down then . . .
11. Listen to the answer and repeatedly ask the question until all the thinking has been generated.
12. Thank the coachee.

Appendix 10

The wheel of life – finding work/life balance

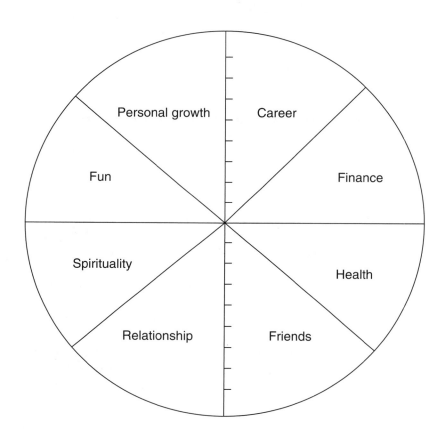

References

Alder, H. (2000) *NLP for Managers: How to Achieve Excellence at Work*. London: Piatkus.

Armstrong, M. (1994) *Performance Management*. London: Kogan Page.

Avolio, B. and Bass, B. (2002) *Developing Potential Across a Full Range of Leadership*. London: Lawrence Erlbaum Associates.

Belbin, R. (1993) *Team Roles at Work*. Oxford: Butterworth-Heinemann.

Blanchard, K., Fowler, S. and Hawkins, L. (2006) *Self-Leadership and the One Minute Manager: Discover the Magic of No Excuses.* London: HarperCollins.

BlessingWhite (2008) *The Coaching Conundrum: Building a Coaching Culture That Drives Organisational Success*. New Jersey: BlessingWhite.

Borg, J. (2010) *Mind Power: Change Your Thinking, Change Your Life*. Harlow, England: Pearson Education Limited.

Bossons, P., Kourdi, J. and Sartain, D. (2009) *Coaching Essentials*. London: A & C Black.

Boyes, C. (2006) *Need to Know NLP?* London: Collins.

Caplan, J. (2003) *Coaching for the Future: How Smart Companies Use Coaching and Mentoring*. London: CIPD.

Caruso, D.R. and Salovey, P. (2008) Coaching for emotional intelligence, in Passmore, J. (ed.) *Psychometrics in Coaching*. London: Kogan Page.

CIPD (Chartered Institute of Personnel and Development) (2004) *Coaching and Buying Coaching Services*. London: CIPD.

CIPD (2005) *Does Coaching Work? A report prepared for the coaching at work conference*. London: CIPD.

CIPD (2007) *Coaching in Organisations: Research Insight*. London: CIPD.

CIPD (2009a) *Taking the Temperature of Coaching.* London: CIPD.

CIPD (2009b) *Innovative Learning and Talent Development: Positioning Practice for Recession and Recovery*. London: CIPD.

CIPD (2010) *Real-World Coaching Evaluation: A Guide for Practitioners*. London: CIPD.

Clutterbuck, D. (2007) *Coaching the Team at Work*. London: Nicholas Brealey.

Cole, M. and Parston, G. (2006) *Unlocking Public Value*. Hoboken, New Jersey: Wiley.

Dattner, B. (2007) *Executive Coaching*. Available from: http//www.dattnerconsulting.com/presetations/executivecoaching.pdf.

Dilts, R.B. (1999). *Sleight of Mouth: The Magic of Conversational Belief Change*. California: Meta Publications.

D'Intino, R.S., Goldsby, M.G., Houghton, J.D. and Neck, C.P. (2007) Self-Leadership: A process for entrepreneurial success. *Journal of Leadership and Organisational Studies*, 13 (4): 105–120.

Dispenza, J. (2007) *Evolve your Brain*: *The Science of Changing Your Mind*. Deerfield Beach, Florida: Health Communications, Inc.

Flaherty, J. (2010) *Coaching: Evoking Excellence in Others*. Oxford: Butterworth-Heinemann.

Fullan, M. (2004) *Leading in a Culture of Change*. San Francisco, California: John Wiley.

Gallwey, T. (1974), in Whitmore, J. (2010) *Coaching for Performance: GROWing Human Potential and Purpose. The Principles and Practice of Coaching and Leadership* (4th edition). London: Nicholas Brealey.

Goleman, D. (2000) *Leadership That Gets Results*. Boston: Harvard Business School Publishing.

Grant, A. (2003) The impact of life coaching on goal attainment, metacognition and mental health. *Social Behavioural and Personality*, 31 (3): 253–264.

Hardingham, A., Brearley, M. and Moorhouse, A. (2009) *The Coach's Coach: Personal Development for Personal Developers*. London: CIPD.

Hawkins, P. and Smith, N. (2010) *Coaching, Mentoring and Organisational Consultancy: Supervision and Development*. Maidenhead: Open University Press.

Heron, J. (1975), in Hawkins, P. and Smith, N. (2010) *Coaching, Mentoring and Organisational Consultancy: Supervision and Development*. Maidenhead: Open University Press.

HM Treasury, Cabinet Office, National Audit Office, Audit Commission, Office for National Statistics (2001) *Choosing the Right Fabric: A Framework for Performance Information*.

Holbeche, L. (2003). *The High Performance Organisation Checklist*. West Sussex: Roffey Park Institute.

Holroyd, J. (2012) *Improving Personal and Organisational Performance in Social Work*. London: Sage.

Holroyd, J. and Brown, K. (2011) *Leadership and Management Development for Social Work and Social Care: Creating Leadership Pathways of Progression*. Bournemouth: Bournemouth University.

I&DᵉA and The Audit Commission (2006) *A Manager's Guide to Performance Management* (2nd edition).

International Coach Federation (2008) Code of Ethics: Definition of Coaching: www.coachfederation.org/icfcredentials/core-competencies.

International Coach Federation (2011) Core Competencies: www.coachfederation.org/icfcredentials/core-competencies.

Johnson, G,. Scholes, K. and Wittington R. (2008) *Exploring Corporate Strategy* (8th edition). Harlow: FT Prentice Hall.

Katzenbach, J. and Smith, D. (1993) *The Wisdom of Teams*. London: McGraw Hill.

Kelan, E., Gratton, L., Mah, A. and Walker, L. (2009) *The Reflexive Generation: Young Professionals' Perspective on Work, Career and Gender*. London: London Business School.

Kilburg, R.R. (2000) *Executive Coaching: Developing Managerial Wisdom in a World of Chaos*. Washington, DC: American Psychological Association.

Kirkpatrick, D. (1998) *Evaluating Training Programs: The Four Levels*. San Francisco, California: Berrett-Koehler Publishers, Inc.

Kirton, M. (2003) *Adaption-Innovation in the Context of Diversity and Change*. London: Routledge.

Kline, N. (2007) *Time to Think: Listening to Ignite the Human Mind*. London: Octopus Publishing Group Ltd.

Kotter, J.P. (1996) *Leading Change*. Boston: Harvard Business School Press.

Kouzes, J.M. and Posner, B.Z. (2007) *The Leadership Challenge* (4th Edition). San Francisco, California: Jossey-Bass.

Ledgerwood, G. (2003) From strategic planning to strategic coaching: Evolving conceptual frameworks to enable changing business cultures. *International Journal of Evidence Based Coaching and Mentoring*, 1 (1): 46–56.

Lee, G. (2007) *Leadership Coaching: From Personal Insight to Organisational Performance*. London: CIPD.

Lennard, D. (2010) *Coaching Models: A Cultural Perspective. A Guide to Model Development for Practitioners and Student Coaching*. London: Routledge.

Lofthouse, R., Leat, D., Towler, C., Hall, E. and Cummings, C. (2010) *Improving Coaching: Evolution Not Revolution*. Nottingham: National College of Leadership of Schools and Children's Services.

Maher, S. (2001) The Case for a Coach. *Association Management*, 53 (4): 78–84.

Manz, C., Neck, C.P., Mancuso, J. and Manz, K.P. (1997) *For Team Members Only: Making Your Workplace Team Productive and Hassle-Free*. AMACOM: American Management Association.

Marr, B. (2009) *Managing and Delivering Performance*. Oxford: Butterworth-Heinemann.

McDermott, I. and Jago, W. (2003) *The NLP Coach: A Comprehensive Guide to Personal Well-Being and Professional Success*. London: Piatkus.

McDermott, I. and Jago, W. (2010) *The Coaching Bible: The Essential Handbook*. London: Piatkus.

McDowall, A. (2008) Using feedback in coaching, in Passmore, J. (ed.) *Psychometrics in Coaching*. London: Kogan Page.

McGovern, J., Lindemann, M., Vergara, M., Murphy, S., Barker, L. and Warrenfeltz, R. (2001) Maximizing the impact of executive coaching: Behavioural change, organisational outcomes, and return on investment. *The Manchester Review*, 6 (1): 1–9.

McHale, M. (2008) *An Evaluation of Executive Coaching as an Intervention Tool from the Coachee's Perspective* – MBA.

McLeod, A. (2009) *Performance Coaching – The Handbook for Managers, HR Professionals and Coaches*. Carmarthen, Wales: Crown Publishing Limited.

McMahon, G. (2001) *Confidence Works – Learn To Be Your Own Life Coach*. London: Sheldon Press.

Megginson, D. and Clutterbuck, D. (2009) *Further Techniques for Coaching and Mentoring*. Oxford: Butterworth Heinemann.

Megginson, D. and Clutterbuck, D. (2010) *Techniques for Coaching and Mentoring*, Oxford: Butterworth Heinemann.

137

Mintzberg, H. (1994) The fall and rise of strategic planning. *Harvard Business Review*, Jan–Feb: 107–114.

Molden, D. (2007) *Managing with the Power of NLP. Neurolinguistic Programming: A Model for Better Management*. London: Prentice Hall Business.

Molden, D. (2010) Coaching models don't work. *Rapport* (Summer): 26–27.

Moore, M. (1995) *Creating Public Value*. Cambridge, Massachusetts: Harvard University Press.

Mullins, L. (1985) *Management and Organisational Behaviour*. London: Pitman.

Neck, C.P. and Manz, C.C. (2009) *Mastering Self-Leadership: Empowering Yourself for Personal Excellence*. Englewood Cliffs, New Jersey: Prentice Hall.

Neill, M. (2009) *Supercoach: 10 Secrets to Transform Anyone's Life*. Carlsbad, California: Hay House.

O'Connor, J. (2001) *NLP Workbook: A Practical Guide to Achieving the Results You Want*. London: Element, HarperCollins.

O'Connor, J. and Lages, A. (2004) *Coaching with NLP: A Practical Guide to Getting the Best Out of Yourself and Others*. London: Element, HarperCollins.

O'Neill, M.B. (2007) *Executive Coaching with Backbone and Heart: A Systems Approach to Engaging Leaders with Their Challenges*. San Francisco, California: John Wiley and Sons, Inc.

Parsloe, E. (1992) *Coaching, Mentoring and Assessing: A Practical Guide to Developing Competence*. London: Kogan Page.

Parsloe, E. (1995) *The Manager as Coach and Mentor: Training Extras*. London: CIPD.

Patterson, K., Grenny, J., McMillan, R. and Switzler, A. (2002) *Crucial Conversations: Tools for Talking when Stakes are High*. Maidenhead: McGraw-Hill.

Pedler, M., Burgoyne, J. and Boydell, T. (2004) *A Manager's Guide to Leadership*. Maidenhead: McGraw-Hill.

Peltier, B. (2010) *The Psychology of Executive Coaching: Theory and Application* (2nd edition). New York: Routledge.

Politis, J.D. (2005). Dispersed leadership predictor of the work environment for creativity and productivity. *European Journal of Innovation Management*, 8 (2): 182–204.

Pratt, J. (2004) *Benefits of Coaching in Business*, White Paper Issue 1. Weymouth: European Coaching Institute.

Rose Charvet, S. (1999) *Words That Change Minds: Mastering the Language of Influence* (2nd edition). Dubuque, Iowa: Kendall/Hunt Publishing Company.

Sale, J. (2011) http://www.motivationalmaps.com [Accessed 2 May 2011].

Scott, C. and Jaffe, D. (1989) *Managing Organisational Change*. London: Kogan Page.

Smither, W., London, M. and Reilly, R.R. (2005) Does performance improve following multisource feedback? A theoretical model, meta-analysis, and review of empirical findings. *Personnel Psychology*, 58 (1): 33–52.

Sparrowe, T.R. (2005) Authentic leadership and the narrative self. *The Leadership Quarterly*, 16: 419–439.

Starr, J. (2011) *The Coaching Manual*. London: Prentice Hall Business.

Stephenson, S. (2009) *Get Off Your 'But': How to End Self-Sabotage and Stand Up for Yourself*. San Francisco, California: Jossey-Bass.

Stone, D., Patton, B. and Heen, S. (1999) *Difficult Conversations*. London: Penguin.

Taffinder, P. (1998) *Big Change: A Route-Map for Corporate Transformation*. Chichester: Wiley.

Tomlinson, H. (1993) Developing professionals. *Education*, 182 (13): 231.

Trotereau, A. (2008) The Generation Y challenge. *Business Digest*, April, 184 (1): 1–8.

Walker, L. (2004) *Changing with NLP: A Casebook of Neurolinguistic Programming in Medical Practice*. Oxford: Radcliffe Medical Press.

Webb, P. (2006) *The Impact of Executive Coaching on Leadership Effectiveness.* New South Wales: Intentional Training Concepts.

Whitmore, J. (2010) *Coaching for Performance: GROWing Human Potential and Purpose. The Principles and Practice of Coaching and Leadership* (4th edition). London: Nicholas Brealey.

Williams, H. (1996) *The Essence of Managing Groups and Teams*. Hertfordshire: Prentice Hall.

Yalom, I. (2002), in Hawkins, P. and Smith, N. (2010) *Coaching, Mentoring and Organisational Consultanc: Supervision and Development*. Berkshire: Open University Press.

Zeus, P. and Skiffington, S. (2001) *A Complete Guide to Coaching at Work*. New York: McGraw Hill.

Zeus, P. and Skiffington, S. (2005) *The Coaching at Work Toolkit: A Complete Guide to Techniques and Practices*. Sydney: McGraw Hill.

Index